The Complete MARTIAL ARTS Catalogue

JOHN CORCORAN
and EMIL FARKAS

SIMON and SCHUSTER　　　NEW YORK

Published by Simon and Schuster
A Division of Gulf & Western Corporation
Rockefeller Center, Simon & Schuster Building
1230 Avenue of the Americas
New York, New York 10020

Designed by Elizabeth Woll
Manufactured in the United States of America

1   2   3   4   5   6   7   8   9   10
1   2   3   4   5   6   7   8   9   10   Pbk.

Library of Congress Cataloging in Publication Data

Corcoran, John, date.
    The complete martial arts catalogue.

    Includes index.
    1. Hand-to-hand fighting, Oriental.   I.   Farkas,
Emil, 1946–   joint author.   II.   Title.
GV1112.C67   796.8'15   77-1636
ISBN 0–671–22668–1
ISBN 0–671–22757–2 Pbk.

ACKNOWLEDGMENTS

The authors wish to express their personal gratitude to Stuart Sobel for his help in coordinating the original manuscript; to Bob Wall, Ed Parker, and Ed Ikuta for permission to use photographs from their personal collections; to Tom Sulak and *Karate Illustrated* for use of the photograph of world superlightweight champion Gordon Franks, as well as for permission to use selected quotes from articles appearing in the magazine; and to Mrs. Linda Lee for overseeing the chapter on her late husband, Bruce Lee. Last, but certainly not least, we wish to express our deep appreciation to members of the editorial and production departments of Simon and Schuster for their presentation of *The Complete Martial Arts Catalogue* in a manner always consistent with their fine house.

CONTENTS

Preface

The influence of Eastern culture on the West is perhaps nowhere more apparent than in our ready acceptance of the Asian martial arts as a common American activity. This acceptance has been accelerated by several events and trends of recent years: Nixon's visit to China; the revival of mysticism, particularly of the Oriental variety; the introduction of acupuncture to modern medical science; the rise of Bruce Lee as the first Chinese-American to reach worldwide superstar status; and the increasing need for protection against violent street crimes.

Now there are several million people in the United States who practice the martial arts as an art and sport. And yet, the martial arts retain a large degree of Oriental mystique. Perhaps that is the most pressing reason for writing a book of this type. Most of the existing books on the subject teach the reader how to execute techniques, but fail to provide adequate answers to the hundreds of questions confronting the neophyte during his early training stages. Non-practitioners also have questions; they have witnessed many variations of the martial arts in television and motion-picture productions, as well as in tournaments and the printed media, and they are intrigued, perhaps, but confused.

This book is based on those questions. It is intended to satisfy the reader's curiosity and give him the answers—even to questions he may never have clearly formulated. It will open the mind to the multifaceted aspects of an Eastern culture which has been mass-marketed on an enormous scale, and yet remains mysterious. The millions of practitioners who have concentrated on but one of the many martial arts will now have an opportunity to read and learn about other, unfamiliar arts. This book will also help separate fact from fiction for the interested layman. Even the thousands of black belts who have spent years perfecting their skills will find this book an invaluable aid for research and a tool with which to supplement the training of their students. It is to these black belts, as well as the millions who will begin to take part in the martial arts within the next few years, that the authors dedicate this book.

Some General Questions About the Martial Arts

Though much has been written about the martial arts, most of this writing has, unfortunately perhaps, focused on the "how-to" phase of learning them. In this book the authors have attempted to inform and educate the reader by, first and foremost, answering the most frequently asked questions pertaining to all aspects of the martial arts. This chapter is designed to dispel the many myths commonly associated with the Oriental fighting arts.

The following questions and answers will clarify subjects as diverse as board breaking, rank, hand conditioning, and self-defense laws, among many other topics. These are but a few of the themes that invite constant questions—questions that the average instructor spends countless hours answering. For that reason alone, instructors will find this chapter a great time-saver if they make it mandatory reading for all their students.

What is the difference between art and sport?

Art, as the word applies to the martial arts, is the specific application of skill in perfect traditional form. Sport, which has come to be considered the antithesis of art, is the specific application of skill to obtain effective results. The practice of one of the martial arts as a sport is not primarily concerned with perfect execution.

How long does it take to earn a black belt?

There is no fixed length of time required to earn a black belt, since the achievement largely depends on the ability of the individual and the amount of time he spends in serious training. The prescribed period for earliest achievement is three years. This, however, is an average. Some outstanding practitioners, like Mike Stone, have earned black belts in as little as six months.

What is a red belt?

There are two variations of the red belt. One, a bright red, is similar to a karate brown belt and is worn directly before obtaining the black belt in the Korean martial arts. The other, a blood-red color, is primarily worn by a 10th-degree master of a style.

Who was Bodhidharma?

Bodhidharma, who is also known as Dot Mor, Tamo, Duruma and Duruma Taishi, was the founder of Zen Buddhism in the sixth century A.D. It is claimed that he traveled from India to China by way of the Himalayas to introduce what is believed to be the first martial art ever practiced in China. It is claimed he taught his martial art in the form of breathing exercises to the monks of the Shaolin Temple. The Shaolin Temple thus became known as the birthplace of the Chinese martial arts.

Why is there so much bowing in the martial arts?

The bow, a traditional gesture of respect, has been used as a formal greeting in Japan for centuries. It is universally used in the Japanese, Korean, and Okinawan martial arts when addressing an instructor or someone of higher rank, and also when entering and leaving the dojo (pronounced *doe*-joe, a gym or karate school). Kung-fu practitioners use various salutations for the same purpose.

Why is breathing so strongly emphasized in the martial arts?

In the martial arts breathing is employed in two ways. In conjunction with the execution of a technique it increases striking power. It is also used for relaxed meditation and while performing dynamic-tension kata (forms). During the dynamic-tension kata (pronounced *caught*-ah), a practitioner tightens his body while going through the form as an assistant strikes him with maximum power on various parts of the body to test his endurance. Without proper breathing, the practitioner could very well be injured during the test. This kata is often used to emphasize the effectiveness of breathing and how it can be employed in actual combat.

What does the term "budo" mean?

"Budo" (pronounced *boo*-doe), meaning to stop conflict, is an encompassing term for the so-called "do" (*doe*) arts such as aikido and judo. These martial arts were formulated in the twentieth century and stem from earlier "ryu" (*ryoo*) arts such as jujutsu-ryu, shorin-ryu, etc. Thus, "budo" is largely used as an umbrella term for all martial arts possessing a name ending with the word "do," which means "way."

The "code of bushido" is often mentioned in the martial arts. What is its importance?

The code of bushido—literally, the way of the warrior—was a code of ethical behavior followed by the samurai warrior. Bushido's main principle was loyalty to one's lord. If a warrior died in the service of his lord, the deed was considered admirable because it was the ultimate expression of his loyalty. Today, bushido provides the ethical background for the martial arts and is claimed to account for such virtues as humility, honor, and discipline.

Which rank certificates are valid?

This has long been a bone of contention. In the early days of the martial arts in America, it was believed that if an Oriental master hadn't signed a rank certificate, it wasn't worth the paper it was printed on. Things have drastically changed, however, because of the worldwide expansion of the martial arts and the many accredited people teaching them. The only way to verify the authenticity of an instructor is to attempt to contact the man or organization responsible for endorsing his certificate. One could also place a call to a national martial-arts publication to determine the instructor's validity.

When did the first boom in the martial arts take place in America?

In 1965, when the late Bruce Lee co-starred in the *Green Hornet* television series.

When facing an opponent on the street, does one want to counter his attack or attack first?

There are many who believe that the best defense is an immediate and effective offense. California's Ed Parker once said, "Those who hesitate meditate in a horizontal position." However, if you were to land the first blow in a street encounter you could very easily find yourself in legal trouble. Self-defense laws favor those who counter a fighting situation, not those who strike first. Unfortunately, many innocent people who have been threatened by an assailant have later paid the consequences if they were foolish enough to initiate the attack, or if they intentionally administered a defense in excess of what the situation called for. For example, if a mugger attacks you with a single punch, you can only counter that punch with enough force to restrain him. If you injure him you could very easily face severe repercussions in court. It has often been said that the self-defense laws are written to protect the criminal and not the victim.

What is a woman's best self-defense weapon if attacked on the street?

Her voice. An ear-piercing scream has deterred many an attacker.

When and where did the martial arts originate?

The answer to this question has plagued historians for centuries. Few documented records exist. There are, however, numerous statues dating back as far as the first century B.C. which depict temple guardians in poses similar to those used in latter-day fighting arts. It is these statues, along with the slight knowledge of the existence of a fighting art called vajramushti, which give rise to the belief that the martial arts may have originated in India. It is further claimed that vajramushti existed in India before 1000 B.C., and was used by the Kshatriya, the warrior class of that period. As far as can be determined, the martial arts passed from India to China around the sixth century A.D., when Bodhidharma introduced a series of breathing exercises to the monks at the famed Shaolin Temple. China was later to develop what is known to the Western world as kung-fu. From China the arts spread to the rest of the world.

Can weightlifting increase martial-arts ability?

Indirectly, it certainly can. The old contention was that weightlifting would cause bulky muscles and thus harm a practitioner's speed. To some extent this is true. However, weightlifting can be compatibly practiced in conjunction with the martial arts in such a way that it will definitely increase striking power without affecting speed. Most claim that the best weight exercises for a martial artist are fast repetitions with light weights. The most recent book written on the subject is *Power Training in Kung-Fu and Karate*. The authors are Leo Fong and Ron Marchini of Stockton, California. The first is a kung-fu and the second a karate practitioner. The book is available through Ohara Publications of Burbank, California.

Weightlifting and martial arts go hand in hand, as amply demonstrated by Franco Columbo, studying here with co-author Emil Farkas. Columbo is one of the world's foremost bodybuilders, and has held the Mr. America and Mr. Universe titles several times.

Why do karate practitioners go barefoot while kung-fu experts wear shoes or boots?

This distinction principally reflects differences in the terrain where the arts were originally practiced centuries ago. Because of rocky and uneven land the Chinese chose to wear shoes to prevent laceration of the feet. On the island of Okinawa, where the art of karate was created, the terrain consisted of soft sand, so the natives as well as karate advocates went without shoes. They did, however, develop tough calluses on the soles of their feet.

What is the most deadly style of the martial arts?

There exists no single style which is considered the deadliest. If there were, presumably everyone would study that particular style, and thus there would be no need for any others. Each particular style has its own inherent advantages and disadvantages. But style only molds a practitioner's basic ability. Once he progresses to a higher level of proficiency it is his individual ability which may or may not make him deadly, not the style he has studied.

Must a black belt register his hands with the police?

In America, this practice has never been necessary. Rumors of such a requirement may have begun because non-practitioners of the martial arts believed it was necessary because the hand conditioning used by some martial artists caused deformed and swollen knuckles, or because professional boxers must register their hands.

It is claimed that there were times in Japan when experts actually had to register their hands at local police stations. There are also stories concerning a similar type of registration for Marines who studied karate on Okinawa. Known for their raucous behavior while on leave, the Marines often took part in some hearty brawls, goes the old story, so the government formulated the registration as a means of deterring continual trouble from the same individuals.

This is one of those venerable rumors that will probably persist for generations despite the efforts of authentic martial artists to stop it.

What is the best method of finding another martial-arts school if one is moving to another state?

Besides the Yellow Pages and the directories contained in the back of most martial-arts magazines, one could consult Bob Wall's *Who's Who in the Martial Arts & Directory of Black Belts*. The first book of its type, it highlights those individuals who have provided positive contributions in all areas of the martial arts, including instruction. If none of the schools or instructors listed is located in the area to which one is moving, then the directory will provide leads to schools all across the United States. The directory is the most accurate and up-to-date listing and contains nearly 5,000 studios. It is published by R. A. Wall Investments of Beverly Hills and can be purchased at any martial-arts supply company.

What is a ninja?

A ninja—literally, an invisible assassin—is a specially trained military spy of ancient Japan. His art, ninjutsu, embraced bushido discipline and numerous martial-arts practices. Japan's feudal period from the late thirteenth to the early seventeenth century served as the setting for the cloak-and-dagger arts of the ninja. Children born into the Iga and Koga systems, both powerful ninjutsu organizations, were trained as spies and remained ninja all their lives. Trainees learned and practiced sophisticated methods of escape. They learned to remain underwater for several minutes at a time, to climb cliffs and walls like human flies, to deceive their pursuers by appearing dead, to displace their joints to slip out of knots when tied, and to predict meteorological conditions such as the santana winds, which they used to their advantage.

A ninja concealed his name, objectives, and techniques, even to the point of death. One never appeared in public without a disguise. For three centuries this devoted band practiced their craft, supplying warlords with a sophisticated sabotage network by which to advance their battles. There are still authentic ninja clans today who practice their craft only to maintain it as a form of cultural martial art.

What are the martial arts?

The martial arts, meaning military, warlike, or fighting arts, include all systems of combat, particularly those stemming from the Asian countries. A martial art, ideally, means any fighting discipline, either with or without the use of weaponry. Each nation has its own specific martial art, or several of them. China's martial art is wu shu, better known to Westerners as kung-fu. The Okinawan martial art is known overall as karate and is subdivided, much like kung-fu, into dozens of branches. Arts like judo and jujutsu, which came before karate, are two of the national martial arts of Japan. Western boxing and wrestling could rightly be called the martial arts of the United States.

Where can one see live performances of the martial arts?

There are many places. Check the local Yellow Pages for schools listed in your area. Many instructors provide demonstrations or a free lesson to potential students. Another excellent exhibition opportunity is a karate tournament. Check your local newspapers for upcoming events, or check the calendar section of any major martial-arts publication for the tourney nearest you. In the past few years, there have also been martial-arts expositions which provide demonstrations exclusively.

Should rank be given to everyone so that students will be encouraged to remain in the martial arts?

No. Martial-arts standards, while slightly flexible, cannot be completely debased without destroying the arts. The martial arts are meant to be a developer of body, mind, and spirit, not a means of pleasing a person's whims. The philosophy behind this position is that the weak person must develop himself, the blind person must learn to sense his opponent's moves, and the person who is crippled or disabled must learn to compensate for his inadequacies. Many individuals, as difficult as it sounds, have achieved success in doing this. A man or woman must rise to the standards of the martial arts to achieve a sense of self-accomplishment. Those who cannot meet the moral standards must be trained or they face their own personal defeat. Those who cannot meet the physical and/or mental standards should practice until they do, and their health will be benefited in the long run. Unfortunately, many instructors bend the rules all too often for various reasons. But the inferior skill of their students then becomes readily apparent. The student is not really benefiting from this practice. Many times, he is only being fooled into believing that he can effectively defend himself.

How much does it cost to join a martial-arts school?

The price varies according to individual studios, but, depending on the amount of down payment, it is usually around $25 to $30 per month. In some cases, this gives a student privileges to use the facilities for five or six days a week, and may include several initial free lessons, a few private lessons, and the regular group sessions. As a rule, however, almost all studios charge an extra fee for private instruction. All newcomers must also purchase a karate uniform, called a gi. Prices range from $15 to $35 depending on the quality of the uniform.

What type of martial-arts school should one look for?

There are two types of operations—commercial and noncommercial. The rates in a commercial school are generally higher for several reasons. The facilities are usually larger, are professionally staffed, and contain the latest in modern training equipment. The noncommercial studio, which may cost as little as $15 per month, is generally smaller, is open only during the evenings, and has fewer instructors and less equipment. In this case, the instructors teach more or less as a sideline, and make their livings elsewhere. This, of course, does not make the school any better or worse.

An interested student should shop around for karate or kung-fu lessons just as he would shop for anything else. Talk with the instructor, observe his classes and the level of skill of his students. Obtain prices and teaching schedules. Don't be afraid to ask as many questions as you feel are necessary. If an instructor fails to answer your questions satisfactorily, or has a lackadaisical attitude, then take your business elsewhere. Keep in mind your personal requirements—self-defense, physical fitness, sport—and when shopping around, look for the school that offers the services you want. Many schools specialize in certain areas. Remember that karate and kung-fu encompass many different styles—hard, soft, linear, circular, etc. Determine the difference and find the one which fits your personal body style and interests. Finally, don't rush into it. Make your decision carefully and objectively.

What is a bushi?

A bushi (pronounced *bush*-ee) is a warrior or samurai. The term is actually an equivalent to samurai but of much earlier origin. It generally referred to mounted warriors or horse soldiers.

What are the Korean, Japanese, and Chinese names for form?

The Korean name is hyung (pronounced as it is spelled), the Japanese name is kata (pronounced *caught*-ah) and the Chinese name is kuen (*koo*-en). Kata is the most widely used. For example, form competition at tournaments is usually referred to as kata competition.

What is sanchin breathing?

Basically, sanchin is forceful breathing with graduated dynamic-tension exercises. It is principally used in certain kata to promote one's ability to absorb punishment. By forcibly breathing and simultaneously tightening the muscles, one is able to absorb blows to various parts of the body. It can rightly be said that the practice of sanchin teaches one to take a punch or kick to the body without harm.

Who were the hwarang warriors?

The hwarang warriors were a band of eighth-century Korean patriots, who, much like the samurai warriors of Japan, adhered to a strict philosophical and moral code of ethics. This clan of soldiers also practiced an early Korean martial art known as hwarang-do, "the way of the flower of manhood."

What is the minimum age for attaining black belt?

In most classical styles of the martial arts a practitioner cannot attain black belt until age sixteen or seventeen. In America, however, children as young as nine have attained the coveted rank. This has primarily been done for publicity purposes since children have neither the ability nor the mentality to uphold such a position.

A noted martial-arts businessman often provides the following analogy. Let's say a qualified black belt can be compared to a properly registered brain surgeon. If a brilliant child genius was able to become a qualified brain surgeon at the age of nine, would you let him operate on you, or would you prefer to have an older surgeon? Obviously, because of his maturity, you would prefer the older surgeon. By the same token, would you as a grown man have a nine-year-old child teach you self-defense?

How many martial-arts masters are there in the United States?

It is extremely difficult to determine the number of authentic martial-arts masters since, unfortunately, too many unqualified people claim this status today. In reality it takes a lifetime, most say sixty years, to become a bona-fide master. Few people really qualify for this esteemed position even though many claim to.

Why are the masters of the martial arts in China so much older than the masters here in the United States?

To be a martial-arts master in China one had to devote a lifetime of study and practice to his art. In America, too many people proclaim themselves masters after a relatively short time (ten or fifteen years). This is the reason for the large number of "young masters" residing in the United States.

What are the names of the Japanese black-belt ranks?

The Japanese black-belt ranks progress from 1 to 10. The numeral signifying each rank precedes the word "dan," meaning "rank." The following list gives the ranks in their respective order from 1st rank to 10th rank: shodan; nidan; sandan; yodan or yondan; godan; rokudan; shichidan; hachidan; kudan; and judan.

What are the names of the Korean black-belt ranks?

The Korean black-belt ranks progress from 1 to 10, just like their Japanese counterparts. The numeral signifying each rank precedes the word "dan," meaning "rank." The following list gives the ranks in their respective order from 1st rank to 10th rank: illdan; yeedan; samdan; sahdan; ohdan; yookdan; childan; paldan; koodan; and shibdan.

What are the names of the Japanese ranks below black belt?

In traditional Japanese karate systems, the ranks below black belt are called kyu (pronounced *cue*), meaning "grade." The kyu ranks progress upward from 8th kyu to 1st kyu. For example, a beginner is automatically an 8th kyu. As he works his way up, he reaches 1st kyu just before gaining black belt and moving into the dan ranks. The kyu ranks follow in their respective order: hachikyu; shichikyu; rokkyu; gokyu; yonkyu; sankyu; nikyu; and ikkyu.

What are the names of the Korean ranks below black belt?

In traditional Korean martial arts the ranks below black belt are called gup (pronounced *goop*), meaning "grade." The gup ranks progress upward from 9th gup to 1st gup. A beginner is a 9th gup. He works his way up to 1st gup, then moves into the dan ranks. The gup ranks follow in their respective order: koogup; palgup; chilgup; yookgup; ohgup; sagup; samgup; yigup; and chogup:

When was the first martial-arts exposition held in the United States?

The first martial-arts expo took place in 1953 when Mas Oyama, founder of the kyokushinkai style of karate, performed publicly at New York's Madison Square Garden. During his U.S. travels that same year, Oyama accepted a challenge to fight a boxer in a public match. The undaunted karate pioneer gave karate its first credible exposure as a practical fighting art when he easily defeated the boxer.

What degree black belt must one be to promote another to black belt?

A black belt must be a senior by two degrees to the person he or she is promoting. For example, one must be a 3rd-degree black belt to promote a student to 1st degree, a 4th-degree black belt to promote a student to 2nd degree, and so forth. Some styles are more lenient and allow promotions by seniors who are advanced over their students by only one degree.

How extensive is the martial-arts training for FBI members?

The FBI Academy trains its agents in hand-to-hand combat instead of in one particular martial art. The method combines practical elements of judo, karate, wrestling, and jujutsu. The objective is to have the agents totally prepared to defend themselves. The training is relatively short, and there is little time to learn the traditional art. The FBI, therefore, prefers to have its agents learn some of the most economical moves from several fighting arts.

Which branch of the U.S. Army was known for its martial-arts training programs?

The Green Berets. This branch of the Armed Forces taught more intricate martial-arts courses than other branches. Their fighting ability was depicted in the motion picture *The Green Berets,* starring John Wayne.

Which branch of the U.S. Armed Forces first recognized the value of martial-arts training?

The Strategic Air Command (SAC), back in the early 1950s, recognized the importance of the martial arts enough to send a team to Japan to study all the different arts and establish similar programs here upon their return. They even imported a group of high-ranking Japanese martial artists of all styles and arts in 1953 to give demonstrations and seminars at various Air Force bases. Judo veteran Mel Bruno of Los Angeles was chiefly responsible for the Air Force's interest in the Oriental combative disciplines.

What are some simple weapons a woman can use for self-defense purposes?

A purse, the edge of a book, keys, a pencil or a pen, the edge of a credit card, or a hat pin. Nearly everything within reach or at her disposal can be transformed into an immediate self-defense item.

If one is attacked by a man wearing glasses, is it ethical to hit him in the face?

While keeping the constraints of self-defense laws in mind, one should try to avoid this action when other maneuvers can be effectively employed. If one's life is in danger, however, it certainly wouldn't be considered less than manly to strike a man in the face who wore glasses. If the man is blinded or badly injured and later files suit, though, he may gain extra sympathy from the court, and damages can be very large.

If a woman is attacked by a man whose intention is to rape her, what are her best defenses?

First, she should scream the word "fire," because more people will respond. Then she should try to hit him as hard as possible in an area which will disable him, such as the groin, the eyes, the knees, or the throat. At the first opportunity, she should run as fast as possible to a safe place.

One of the most efficient means of disabling a male attacker is to kick him in one of the weaker areas of the body, such as behind the knee.

What is the best self-defense method to use when attacked by a dog?

The most important defense is the victim's first move. He should extend his forearm, so that the dog grasps it in his teeth rather than biting any other part of the body. This takes intestinal fortitude, as it is difficult to sacrifice any part of the body knowing it will be injured. The victim should then immediately strike the dog on the nose as hard as possible. This method has been used effectively. The Armed Forces teach a less humane method which is not usually necessary unless a dog is trained to kill its prey. After extending the arm as the point of contact, and once the dog has a firm grasp, the victim places his other hand around and behind the dog's neck and bends sharply forward, breaking the dog's neck. This method is uncalled for in a normal situation.

What type of martial-arts training do Armed Forces personnel receive?

None of the Armed Forces offers a specific type of martial art to its recruits. Recruits do, however, receive a hand-to-hand combat course consisting of a combination of judo, wrestling, karate, and jujutsu, among other fighting disciplines. For recruits who want to pursue further martial-arts training, most bases have established judo or karate clubs. The Air Force is especially noted for its high-caliber judo players, many of whom have gone on to win national and international fame. On the other hand, the Marines have been acknowledged for producing high-caliber karate fighters. World heavyweight karate champion Joe Lewis received his early training in the Marines while stationed on Okinawa.

What are some of the major reasons why people study the martial arts?

People take up instruction in the martial arts for many individual reasons. Some of the principal reasons are self-defense, physical fitness, the relief of stress and achievement of mental calmness, philosophy, and the pursuit of a tournament career in the sport.

How is physical fitness related to the martial arts?

Martial-arts training promotes isometric and isotonic exercises. All training, however, in martial arts as well as in other physical activities, is based on the development of the cardiovascular system for endurance. To achieve long-range endurance one must perform strenuous exercises repetitiously. The unique point about martial-arts training is that one not only achieves self-defense skills, but simultaneously, one achieves varying states of physical fitness depending on the degree of exercises. This dual benefit has attracted thousands of practitioners to the arts, and continues to attract new students who do not want to exercise just for the sake of exercising.

Why are there so few injuries in the martial arts?

There are few injuries in most martial arts, with the exception of perhaps judo and full-contact karate, because all techniques are pulled short of their respective targets in practice. Even in the amateur ranks of sport karate, all techniques are pulled, and it has even come to be called noncontact. Practitioners have found this to be the safest practice method, which also accounts for the martial arts being considered a wholesome family activity. Of course, one encounters the minor injuries found in any athletic endeavor—bruises, sprains, and brushburns. In judo, the first thing one learns is the method of falling without injury. Once the students are secure in this, only then do they engage in throwing one another. Because of this great emphasis on safety precautions, few major injuries ever occur.

It has been said that the great philosopher Plato wrote about a martial art. Is this true?

Yes, according to information contained in the out-of-print book *The History of American Karate.* In this passage from *Laws* (approximately 350 B.C.), Plato mentioned an early Greek martial art similar to karate: "The war-dance has a different character, and may properly be called the Pyrrhic; it depicts the motions of eluding blows and shots of every kind by various devices of swerving, yielding ground, leaping from the ground or crouching, as well as contrary motions which lead to a posture of attack, and aim at the reproduction of the shooting of arrows, casting of darts, and dealing of all kinds of blows. In these dances the upright, well-braced posture which represents the good body and good mind, and in which the bodily members are in the main kept straight, is the kind of attitude we pronounce right, that which depicts their contrary, wrong."

Whether or not the Pyrrhic or pankration, another Greek art, had any influence on the fighting techniques of Asia is a matter for speculation. However, Plato's description of the Pyrrhic might well be used to describe the modern karate kata (form) or formal exercise.

What is the oldest martial art known to man?

The early Greek martial art of pankration (pan-*kray*-shin) is believed by many historians to have been the first "total" fighting discipline known to man. John Corcoran, co-author of this book, uncovered a rare book in 1976 which provided substantial evidence of the existence of pankration as a pre-Christian form of sport and combat. "Pankration," sometimes spelled "pancration" or "pankratium," literally means "all powers." It is an ancient fighting form in which every physical and mental resource—hands and feet, mind and spirit—are combined in all-out combat. Pankration was developed as a combination of the earlier forms of boxing and wrestling practiced by the Greeks.

While some historians seem content to trace the origins of the martial arts to the Indian vajramushti system, one thing that can be noted is that pankration and Pyrrhic, the early Greek war-dance similar to modern karate kata, both antedate the Indian statues depicting temple guards in poses similar to those used in latter-day fighting arts.

In 648 B.C., the pankration was officially entered into the Olympic Games, almost a century after the founding of the Olympics in ancient Greece. Further evidence of the existence of pankration is found in ancient vases and paintings depicting warriors engaging in competitive combat, as well as in direct quotes from works of noted philosophers and poets of ancient Greece.

Should you keep your eyes fixed on your opponent when bowing?

If you don't, theoretically, you could be struck unexpectedly, but nonetheless appropriately, at that point. While the bow is a gesture of respect it is still traditionally performed from the waist. And although the upper body dips with the bow, the eyes never fail to intently study the opponent's face. Then, if he did· decide to attack at this opportune moment, one could be alerted by his facial expressions or threatening body movements.

Is there a unique way of tying the belt worn in the martial arts?

Yes. It is called a flat reef or double square knot. The belt is tied by wrapping it around the gi or uniform twice, then tucking one end of the belt under the double thickness of the part at the front. Then, when the knot is tied, it holds both parts of the belt together.

What is the first thing one learns in a martial-arts school?

Principally, to bow when entering the training area. A new student is usually taught this act first because, upon entering the studio to enroll, he or she is given a tour of the facilities. As the student takes this tour, he is generally told to bow when entering the training area even though he is not yet a full-fledged student.

When you are sparring and your belt comes undone, what is the proper procedure?

Traditionally, you call time and turn around, facing away from your opponent as you retie your belt. When this occurs while practicing in a strict, formal dojo, you must kneel down on one knee while turned around and retying your belt.

What does the word "os" mean?

There are several literal translations for the word "os" (pronounced *oos*): "good morning"; "request"; "entreat"; "push ahead." Some authorities claim the word is a contraction of *ohayo-gozaimas,* meaning "good morning." Others say it is a contraction of *onegai-shimas,* meaning "to request" or "entreat." However, most claim the term is an expression taken from the *osu* or "push" used in sumo wrestling. Hence, os is commonly understood to mean "push ahead" or "never give up." As such, it is a common greeting in Japanese karate circles.

What is a kiai?

The kiai (pronounced *key*-eye), meaning spirit meeting, is a loud shout or yell of self-assertion commonly employed in numerous martial arts. There are two purposes of the kiai. One is to startle an opponent, since loud noises are known to momentarily alarm any human being, and thus interrupt his thought processes. This provides the user of the kiai with an initial advantage to land an important blow. The second purpose of the kiai is to reinforce a technique and maximize body strength through the expulsion of air. This concentrated expulsion, when used properly, can also tighten the body in order to absorb the shock of any body blow the user may receive.

How is the Shaolin Temple associated with the martial arts?

It was an actual monastery located in the Hunan Province of China about 1,400 years ago. It is considered the birthplace of the Chinese martial arts, since Bodhidharma of India introduced a series of breathing exercises there. The temple was later burned to the ground.

Which is the oldest karate school in the United States?

According to Arizona's Robert Trias, he opened his dojo in Phoenix in 1946. As far as can be determined, it was the very first karate school to open its doors in America.

Where is the largest karate school in America located?

Although it has yet to be determined which school is actually the largest, there are quite a few contenders for the prestigious position. The Olympic Center, operated by Joseph Artesi in New Jersey, sits on 34 acres of land and comes complete with swimming pool and track. In view of the entire property, Artesi's Olympic Center is probably the largest martial-arts-related training facility in the United States. In New York City, the largest commercial dojo is run by Yoshiteru Otani. It has a 32,000-square-foot workout area. In Vestal, New York, Hidy Ochiai has an expansive facility constructed specifically for teaching karate. Jhoon Rhee of Washington, D.C., is also said to have one of the largest karate schools in the country. Another of the largest is the new Chuck Norris karate studio in Virginia Beach.

Who is the oldest living practitioner of the martial arts?

One of the oldest known living practitioners is Hohan Soken, eighty-seven, of Okinawa. The master still practices daily, and, along with his protégé Fusi Kesei, runs his worldwide shorin-ryu karate organization.

What is the most frequently asked question in the martial arts?

In reality, there are about a dozen questions which every new student asks. The one specific question which appears to be asked most frequently, however, is "How long does it take to make the rank of black belt?"

Why are karate uniforms made of lightweight fabric while judo uniforms are very heavy?

The judo gi (uniform) is constructed of heavy cotton and canvas material because it has to withstand severe tugging at the lapels where judo players grip to execute many of their throws. Since there are few throws used in karate, there is no need for excessively heavy material in the gi, although some of them are made of 100-percent cotton for durability and a snapping effect when executing kicks and punches.

Are contract schools better than non-contract martial-arts schools?

No. Since there have been no quality controls established in the martial-arts industry, a school can be judged only on individual merits. Maintain caution when signing contracts unless the school has been in business for many years in your community. There are such things as fly-by-night outfits which sign students to stiff contracts, then fold up soon afterward and sell the contracts to a local finance company for collection.

One method of checking whether or not the school or its instructor is reputable is to write or call an established martial-arts magazine. The editors are usually acquainted with the more reputable martial-arts business owners. Contract schools can be considered a better buy if you can afford the higher rates. They are usually professionally staffed, feature modern training equipment, and are open twelve hours per day, six days per week. Many of the non-contract dojo are open only on a part-time basis.

Why do the majority of women take up the martial arts?

According to female karate pioneer Pauline Short of Portland, Oregon, "Most women are studying the martial arts for self-defense, physical conditioning, and to increase their self-assertiveness. It is not a passing fad for them and many intend to practice indefinitely; most are committed for life."

More and more, women are also moving into the sport aspect of karate, and champions are being born in both sparring and form competition. It appears clear, however, that the most important reason that women have become interested in the martial arts is the dire need for self-protection against the rising crime rate and growing number of rape assaults.

Most women study the martial arts for self-defense, for physical conditioning, and to increase their self-assertiveness. The rising crime rate and number of rape assaults has increased the appeal of the martial arts for women.

Does rank mean anything after black belt?

Yes, though many times it has little to do with actual performance ability. Instead, after gaining 1st-degree black belt, the individual advances in rank according to his or her knowledge of the art. In most styles, once an accomplished individual reaches 5th-degree black belt, the remaining black-belt ranks to 10th-degree are merely honorary.

Should children and adults be instructed together in the same classes?

Formerly they often were, but recently, more and more instructors are separating their students according to age groups. This seems to have been a very sensible move, since mature adults can comprehend knowledge more readily than adolescents. Children encounter special learning problems because their attention span is severely limited, so instructors have incorporated strict, disciplined games in which youngsters can have fun as they learn. Adults, being more willing to undertake the repetitious practice required to learn martial-arts skills, prefer participating with others of the same age groups. Many older students who are seeking self-defense expertise rather than skill in competition find this arrangement encouraging because they aren't expected to work out as strenuously as people in their athletic prime.

At which age should children begin studying the martial arts?

Opinions vary from age five to thirteen. In special cases, children as young as five have successfully adapted to the study of the Oriental fighting disciplines. Of course, every proud parent feels that his youngster, no matter how young, is vastly talented. What it appears to boil down to is motivation, from both the parents and the instructor. If motivation and interest are maintained, the young student will be less likely to drop out. But in all cases, if a youngster isn't really interested in the first place he will most likely practice halfheartedly, and thus obtain mediocre results.

How many martial-arts schools are there in the United States?

According to Bob Wall's *Directory of Black Belts,* the most recent figures show nearly 5,000 studios across the country.

Which state has the most martial-arts schools from which to choose?

By far, California, and more specifically, Southern California. There are 1,212

Children of five and up can become proficient in karate. Both girls and boys, if properly motivated, can become adequately skilled in any of the martial arts.

studios throughout the entire state, with the largest concentration in the Los Angeles area and the second largest in the San Francisco area. The second-ranking state is New York, with the principal concentration in the New York City area.

What is the oldest age at which one should enter the martial arts?

There is no age limit. The middle-aged and the elderly have reaped various benefits from practicing the martial arts. In fact, some karate tournaments feature special noncontact divisions for participants forty years and over. A prime example of the nonexistence of an upper age limit occurred when Senator Milton R. Young of North Dakota used his karate skills to become reelected to a fifth term. The most telling campaign argument against the popular Young was that he was too old. The word was spread that by the end of his term, Young would be eighty-three, and perhaps not vigorous enough to serve the needs of North Dakota. But mysteriously, photos began to appear around the state showing

Young in karate stances—kicking, punching, and jumping—and North Dakotans decided that Young, indeed, was still young enough for them.

How do the martial arts rate as an American industry?

According to the September-October 1974 issue of *City* magazine (of San Francisco), the martial arts as a business was worth about $60,750,000. *City's* figures were the products of informed guesses obtained by calling leading martial-arts businessmen for estimates in their respective areas. The estimates were then averaged and totaled to arrive at the above figure. The total figure includes revenue from "bubble-gum stuff—Bruce Lee T-shirts, posters, GI Joes with kung-fu grip, and Shang Chi, Master of Kung-Fu comic books; income from all spectator events—tournaments, demonstrations, TV panel talkies, and traveling road shows; private instruction, police and armed forces training, and the income from international distribution of TV's Kung Fu series for broadcast in 42 countries." The $60,750,000 quoted by *City* excluded foreign markets such as Southeast Asia, where Bruce Lee films broke all records; Japan, where judo, karate, and kendo are taught in public schools and colleges as are baseball and football here; Hong Kong, where the Shaw brothers, moguls of martial-arts moviedom, hold a family fortune estimated to be at least $200,000,000 and perhaps five times as much. Thus, *City's* estimate is conservative. Chances are the figure is much higher.

Why is discipline necessary in martial-arts training?

Primarily because the martial arts can be mastered only by controlled obedience and repetitious training. It is extremely difficult for the average person to maintain enough self-discipline to face the exasperating grind required to perfect any athletic skill. Thus, martial-arts instructors have always taught in a disciplinary fashion. Long before the Asian fighting arts reached their current commercialized status, the training had developed an almost religious quality.

How important is size in learning the martial arts?

Size bears no distinct advantage in individual practice in a school. A small man, however, can usually respond more easily to the physical exertion required. But it all depends on individual conditioning and athletic background. For example, a person who has been inclined toward athletics finds the martial arts easier to master. In noncontact sport karate, where all blows are pulled short of the target, a lighter or smaller person many times has defeated someone larger because the rules are set up in such a way that the first one to score points can generally win the match. Thus, speed is the most important factor, which in turn gives the edge to the smaller fighter. However, in full-contact competition, where an individual is pitted against someone close to his own weight, it largely becomes a matter of who is the better fighter. Therefore, full-contact is based on skill and physical conditioning. It is not recommended nor is it mandatory for everyone to learn full-contact.

Is it true that some martial-arts masters can dodge bullets?

No. Some of the mythology of the martial arts has been much exaggerated by those seeking publicity.

Is it true that some martial artists can dodge arrows?

Yes, but there is a trick to this feat. Unknown to the audience, the deception lies in the skill of the man shooting the arrows. With enough practice it is possible to determine by silent count exactly when the archer will release the arrow. The archer can also emit a noise a fraction of a second before release, and, if the distance is sufficient, the martial artist can evade the arrow with room to spare. In the few public demonstrations of this type, the arrows usually bore blunt tips. There has been one demo reported, however, where a martial-arts performer actually caught the arrow in flight! Such exhibitions are performed only to demonstrate the quick reflexes gained in martial-arts training.

Can the handicapped learn the martial arts?

Yes. It has been proved over and over again that anyone can learn the martial arts if his will to do so is strong enough to overcome physical, emotional, or mental handicaps. Of course, the educational approach must be relevant to the situation, and thus requires extreme patience on the part of both the instructor and his or her students. There have been cases where the martial arts have proved to be very valuable therapy. Some of the handicapped who have benefited from its practice have been blind, mentally retarded, or deaf, and others have had arms or legs amputated.

According to prominent martial-arts journalist Massad Ayoob in a report to *Karate Illustrated Magazine,* the martial arts are "a very healthful form of physical therapy with one advantage conventional 'PT' [physical training] sadly lacks: it is interesting enough to keep an already depressed patient involved long enough for it to work. Boredom is the greatest enemy of conventional exercise therapy and the martial arts handily circumvent it. For handicapped children, especially boys, it provides an area of macho achievement that is desperately needed. As builders of physical strength and personal confidence in people starving for both, the martial arts have perhaps no peer."

What is the Martial Arts for the Handicapped Federation?

Preston Carter of Trenton, New Jersey, a paraplegic, founded the unique organization in April 1974. Among its members are Ed Velarde, a polio victim, and Ted Vollrath, a double leg amputee. The federation appointed Charles Bonet, who has no physical impairments, as its chief instructor. MAHF is chartered as a nonprofit organization, whose purpose is to make available specialized martial-arts training for handicapped people of all kinds: those with breathing problems, those unable to walk or move their limbs properly, the blind, and the congenitally deformed.

Are Orientals more adaptable to the martial arts?

That's like asking if Muhammad Ali is more adaptable to boxing because he is black. Race holds no advantage or importance in learning and practicing the martial arts, though Orientals share a long heritage of having founded them. That's why many of the martial arts are also referred to as Asian fighting disciplines. Because they are readily adaptable by any race, the martial arts have spread worldwide and are practiced by millions.

Can black belts, like movie stars, insure their hands for large sums of money?

A person can insure just about anything with Lloyd's of London. But because the risk of injury to the hands is so much greater than, say, it is to a movie star's legs, the premiums would be astronomical. To this date, no known martial artist has ever insured his or her hands.

How quickly can one learn the martial arts?

It definitely depends on individual ability and the amount of time invested in actual practice. There are no shortcuts to developing proficiency. To become basically effective, it is believed the average person has to spend at least six months in consecutive training of about five days per week.

Which is the quickest martial art one can learn?

None of them. All require the same expenditure of energy and self-discipline.

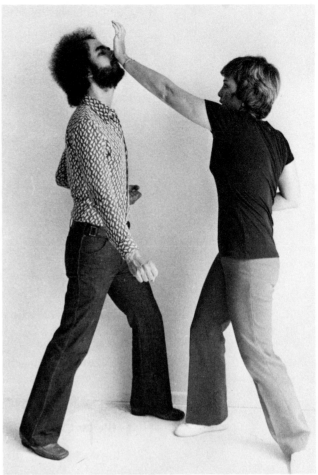

If an adversary attempts to attack, block his attacking hand as shown in the first photo, and quickly deliver a palm heel strike to the bridge of the nose.

Does one need any special physical skills to learn the martial arts?

No. However, it has been found that those who possess natural athletic skills adapt to the physical training with relative ease.

What are some of the weaker parts of the body which a woman can strike when attacked?

As Bruce Lee once advised, strike the groin, poke at the eyes, and kick to the shin, groin, or knee. Other areas more susceptible to counterattack are the tip of the nose when the palm is thrust upward; the collarbone, which requires very little pressure to break; the ears, clapped with both hands; and the instep, stamped with enough force and accuracy. It is best to practice these moves to acquire pinpoint accuracy so that in an attack, a woman can more readily adapt to the situation.

Is biting permitted in a fight?

In any street encounter where it becomes a matter of life or death, or even personal injury, there are no rules regulating combat. By all means, take any opportunity to bite.

Is it dishonorable to kick someone in the groin?

In the old days, anyone who kicked an opponent automatically was considered a dirty fighter. Today, fighting has become a sophisticated study and it is no more dishonorable to kick someone in the groin than it is to strike him in the face.

Is it cowardly to run when attacked?

Not at all. The faster you run, the faster you could avoid an embarrassing or painful encounter. One should always try to avoid a confrontation.

What's the best way to avoid a fight?

Try to persuade the attacker not to follow through. When you have no choice, it is advised that you hit first and hit hard so that your first move will disable the assailant.

Why are there so few female black belts?

Because most women study the martial arts only to learn enough basic knowledge to defend themselves adequately. Most do not enter the martial arts with the intention of becoming a black belt.

How many people in the United States have studied the martial arts?

Unfortunately, the last primary poll taken by *Black Belt Magazine* was for 1972, which doesn't truly reflect the tremendous growth brought about by the martial-arts-movie explosion. Another important factor to consider is the gross dropout rate. Some instructors contend that the turnover rate of beginners in the first three months is as high as 90 percent. That being the case, it is estimated that the figures acquired by *Black Belt* could be conservatively multiplied by seven, which would represent only a 70-percent turnover.

Black Belt reported the following: "The year 1972 set the stage for a dramatic upsurge of interest in the field of martial arts. Karate again took the lead, with its membership (including kung-fu practitioners) growing from 148,000 in 1971 to 164,800 in 1972, an increase of 16,000 (or 10 percent). Statistics on growth of the various karate styles for the past year are: Okinawan: Gained 32,000; increased from 14,000 in 1971 to 46,000 in 1972. Japanese: Lost 6,000; decreased from 50,000 to 44,000. Korean: Lost 7,000; decreased from 75,000 to 68,000.

"Youngsters below the age of 14 continue to flock to karate schools around the nation. From 36,200 in 1971, an additional 5,900 youngsters have entered karate schools. In this age of Women's Lib, it is not surprising to find that women have also increased their interest in this art of self-defense. From the total of 164,800 participants, 42,000 are youngsters, 29,000 are women, 93,700 are men. For 1972, only 6,800 empty-hand practitioners were kung-fu followers. This rediscovered art form attracted 900 females and another 900 youngsters below the age of 14. Kung-fu's magnetic attraction will be even greater in the future due to current emphasis by the television and motion picture industries. A whopping 8,100 black belts were actively engaged in karate in 1972.

"Judo has not significantly increased its ranks in 1972. The number of practicing judoka decreased by 700, from 39,000 in 1971 to 38,300 in 1972. [However, *Black Belt* admitted that the survey was taken when many judo schools had closed for summer vacation. Many high school and college clubs were inactive at the time.] Women judoka increased by 900 participants, from 6,500 in 1971 to 7,400 in 1972. Judoka 14 and under increased by 3,000, from 15,600 in '71 to 19,500 in '72.

"Aikido has grown from 3,700 to 1971 to 7,900 in 1972, an increase of 4,200. The popularity of aikido grows at a slower pace for many reasons. Aikido dojo are not known to advertise their art. It is an intriguing art form that interests many adults because of its philosophical approach and concentration of mind development. Unfortunately, not many people are aware of this art form. . . .

"The apparent trend for jujitsu is downward with no significant increase seen for the near future. The two largest judo organizations are converting some jujitsu practitioners to judo. In addition, jujitsu, like aikido, does not have any form of competition and therefore does not reach the public as karate and judo do."

Bob Wall's *Who's Who in the Martial Arts & Directory of Black Belts*, published in September 1975, reported that there were close to 5,000 martial-arts studios in operation across the nation. But many schools had already closed following the economic crisis and the martial-arts-movie boom in late 1974 and early 1975.

A secondary poll was taken by the Professional Karate Association in 1975, and it reflects much more accurately the significant increase in martial-arts activities during the kung-fu boom. The Professional Karate Association's report states: "The high-level interest in the martial arts is mirrored in the number of magazines published about them. There are 13 active martial arts magazines, four of which have a readership as follows: (1) *Action Black Belt*, published by M.F. Enterprises, Inc., 85,000; (2) *Black Belt Magazine*, published by Rainbow Publications, 120,000 readers; (3) *Karate Illustrated,* also published by Rainbow Publications, 85,000 readers; (4) *Masters of Self-Defense,* published by Country-wide Communications, Inc., with 125,000 readers. Magazine publishers report that there is a great demand for these magazines, and that related items, such as comic books, also move very well.

"The true measure of the martial arts, however, is in the number of people actively involved. In 1962, there were 600 judo clubs and 20,000 participants in the United States. That number has now grown by more than 10 times: at present, more than 250,000 people have gone through or are undergoing a study of judo. At least 165,000 additional people have studied or are studying in a studio or school one of the other martial arts, such as karate or aikido.

"Of the 250,000 people who have studied judo, 20%, or 50,000 of them are women. The women's liberation movement, coupled with the ever-rising crime rate, has been another significant factor in the growth of the martial arts.

"A final indication of the growth of the martial arts is the size of the equipment market. This equipment includes mats, uniforms, and self-protective equipment. The majority of the equipment is made in Japan by private companies, such as the Tokaido Co., although Costello, in New York, is one American company which makes uniforms. Distribution is handled by martial arts supply companies who sell to schools and studios. Industry sources estimate the total size of the market at 100 million dollars. The meaning of this figure can be seen by comparing it with other sports equipment markets: the entire tennis equipment market, considered large, is valued at $280 million, while the entire ping-pong market, considered small, is valued at $40 million.

"The martial arts are a new field, but their level of popularity ensures that they will be a major force in athletics soon. The market has grown in 10 years from under 50,000 to presently over 400,000 students. And these students represent a complete demographic spectrum, young, old, and middle-aged, male and female, the low to high income brackets, professions from business executive to house-wife. This broad and solid interest base assures the martial arts an even larger market in the years to come."

Why should women study the martial arts?

In today's crime-ridden society, a woman never can tell when she may need to use self-defense skills. More and more, women are also realizing the beneficial aspects of body toning, trimming, and overall health that can be derived from the martial arts.

What are the comparative fighting abilities of men and women?

In a report in the April 1976 issue of *Karate Illustrated,* authors Donnie Williams and Ron Goodman made the following analysis: "In this article, when we say fighting, we're going to be talking about the real thing: survival fighting, true blood-and-guts, survival of the fittest, anything goes, nothing barred, street and back alley and barroom kill-or-be-killed. We are not talking about sparring or competition.

"Three things determine the effectiveness of a fighter. The first two of these are mental/emotional, the third is partly mental and partly physical. In order, they are confidence, desire and ability." Of these three categories, no significant advantage was accorded to members of either sex. However, the report further stated, "The two areas where the abilities of men and women are decidedly *not* equal is power. How hard can you hit with your hands and feet, and how much force do your blocks have to stop a punch, strike or kick coming at you? This is affected by speed and technique, as well as by actual muscular strength. However, we have already determined in the areas of technique and speed, there is no significant difference between the sexes. Therefore, with the other two factors equal, power *will* depend on pure muscular strength.

"The conclusion we draw from all this is that the female fighter is going to be at a very considerable disadvantage in striking and defensive power as opposed to her male opponent, particularly in the upper body." (It was earlier stated by the authors that a man's leg muscles are, normally, about twice as strong as his arm muscles, while a woman's legs are more like four times as strong as her arms. They therefore concluded that the wise female fighter will work extensively on her kicks and rely on them against a male attacker.)

"Finally, there is the matter of durability, the ability to absorb physical punishment from one's opponent and go on fighting at top level. In the opinion of experienced martial artists, it is believed that women, due to lighter bones and musculature, are less capable of taking the same pounding men are. A body punch that will be easily absorbed by a well-conditioned 160-pound male can be extremely painful to a 120-pound female."

So, the authors found very significant differences only in the areas of muscular strength and ability to absorb physical punishment. "These factors may mean relatively little in [noncontact] tournament competition," claim the authors, "but can be vital in a street situation. However, we have also found that a properly trained female martial artist, who uses her training well, has a very good chance of winning such an encounter with a male street attacker."

Is it possible to learn the "true" martial arts?

Since the introduction of the Asian fighting arts in America, there has been a tendency for some people to believe that their particular style of martial art is the only "true" way to practice, or the only "true" system. However, even their definitions of the word "true" have greatly conflicted, largely establishing the concept that truth lies in the belief of the individual practitioner, regardless of style. Since the martial arts are geared toward individual development, every advocate feels he is learning the "true" way.

Who is the "best" martial artist?

No one single person has proven to be best, although many have branched out to become extremely proficient at one or two aspects of the Oriental fighting arts. As the old saying goes, "No matter how good you are, there's always someone better." Considering the multitudinous aspects of the martial arts, it is impossible for one person to stand out as the "best" over everyone else.

Why do martial artists use meditation?

Meditation is part of the martial arts because the arts are mental as well as physical disciplines. One must learn to calm his mind. A person relaxed and calm will be a more capable fighter. It's a common fact that tenseness hinders speed. In the dojo, meditation is usually practiced both before and after class, first to calm the mind for the approaching training session and to dispel irrelevant thoughts, and then after the session to relax the body.

Why are the martial arts considered defensive arts?

The martial arts were developed to a large degree by oppressed people who were prohibited from bearing arms. This has been stressed to such a degree that, in karate, most kata begin and end with a block, typifying the defensive attitude.

The Art of Karate

The art of karate didn't exactly burst onto the American scene, as some enthusiasts would have you believe. The fact is, it's been here since 1946, when a U.S. sailor named Robert Trias opened the first known karate school in Phoenix, Arizona. It then took some twenty years before the art captured the wide attention of the American public, and perhaps five more before karate became a household word.

Nevertheless, because of its esoteric origins and the tremendous variations of its uses and benefits, karate continues to be largely misunderstood by the average person. There are those who still insist karate is an art of board and bone breaking; others maintain the belief that a black belt must register his or her hands with the local authorities. Still others tend to avoid its practice, thinking karate is too deadly or unsafe for the average person.

The following chapter will help to dispel the misconceptions associated with the art and practice of karate, and, at the same time, explain its various facets of physical fitness, self-defense, philosophy, and scientific strategies.

Of the customary ten ranks of black belt in karate, how many are awarded according to physical ability?

In most cases, 6th- to 9th-degree black belt are strictly honorary and are usually awarded over lengthy periods of time. The 10th-degree black belt, the highest rank in karate, is generally passed on from the master of a style to his immediate protégé.

Breaking in karate, which can be used as a method of testing power, is primarily used today in demonstrations because of its sensational effect. Here Tak Kubota smashes several bricks with his fist.

Are breaking boards and bricks important in karate?

To some degree, breaking objects serves a purpose. While it has been principally used in demonstrations because of its sensational effect, its practicality lies in the fact that it can be employed as a test of a practitioner's strength or power. And even though it has been effectively applied as a display of showmanship, most purportedly difficult feats can be accomplished by an inexperienced neophyte once he has learned the principles behind breaking.

How difficult is it to break bricks and boards?

The degree of difficulty in board or brick breaking depends primarily on the size and tensile strength of each object. If the boards are first warmed in an oven to completely rid them of excess moisture and are then forcibly struck in the direction of the grain, they will break much more easily. This, of course, depends on the number of boards used, since the difficulty increases as more boards are added.

In breaking bricks, an excess of sand, an ingredient which composes many types of bricks, markedly decreases the degree of difficulty. The more sand the easier the brick is to break.

What is the most difficult object to break?

A round stone has generally appeared to present the most difficulty.

What are the belt ranks in karate?

When karate originated, all belts were white. Since the belt was never washed, it gradually became black over a period of years from accumulation of soil and sweat. When the colored-belt system was instituted it followed tradition by having its color become darker as a student advances in rank. In traditional karate schools the principal belt colors or ranks are white (beginner), green, then brown (both intermediate), and black (advanced). In the commercial karate schools across America, the colors used are white, yellow, and orange (beginner), blue, green, and purple (intermediate), brown (advanced intermediate), and black.

There is a great variety of styles in karate, so it is difficult to determine if absolutely everyone uses the above methods. They are, however, the most common.

Karate students are often seen performing strange dances. What are these dances, and are they really necessary for someone learning to fight?

The so-called dances are known as kata (*caught*-ah) and are used as the formal exercises of karate as well as in many other martial arts. There are two schools of thought concerning the usefulness of kata. Traditionalists believe that without kata, there is no karate. They claim it is the backbone of karate and the foundation encompassing all of its mental and physical principles—including actual fighting against an opponent. The other faction, composed of what can be called open stylists, claim that kata is a waste of time because it holds no actual resemblance to modern fighting. They claim further that because the techniques used in the shadowboxing method were created centuries ago, the moves lack realism in dealing with contemporary combat problems. However, extremists on both sides of the issue agree that there is a happy medium. One can practice enough kata to develop certain basic assets such as balance, precision, speed, and power. And by practicing actual sparring against an opponent one can enhance timing, endurance, ability to take a punch, and overall combat effectiveness.

What are the major differences between Japanese, Okinawan, Chinese, and Korean stylists?

Today, there has been a general tendency to learn techniques from all styles in order to become more well-rounded. Therefore, it is sometimes difficult to determine the exact style of any particular practitioner. However, the major char-

New York's Fred Miller demonstrates a kata (form), which many masters consider the foundation of the martial arts.

acteristics of each style can be perceived, even by the untrained eye. Japanese stylists tend to move in linear paterns, and many of the Japanese-style techniques are formed by straight lines. Okinawans, who formulated karate from kung-fu, use the same type of linear patterns but they also incorporate, to some degree, the circular blocks often associated with Chinese stylists. A practitioner of the Korean styles can be identified much more readily because of the emphasis on spectacular kicks. Korean stylists will kick 90 percent of the time instead of using their hands. A Chinese stylist is the easiest to identify. He or she wears a different type of uniform altogether, as well as boots or soft shoes. Chinese techniques are smoother and more graceful, and are complemented by many low stances and circular hand patterns.

Does a karate expert warn an adversary of his capabilities?

A karate expert, in most instances, is required by law to warn an opponent of his superior abilities, but in reality, there is seldom enough time to do so. A black belt is often compared to a professional boxer, regardless of his individual ability and the fact that he may not be a professional fighter. Therefore, in the eyes of the law he is considered to have a distinct advantage over the average mugger.

Unfortunately, when this type of notification is used it provokes the assailant in two ways. He will either laugh outright, thinking that you may be trying to avoid the situation out of fear; or he will launch a more determined attack just in case you happen to be telling the truth. The warning, according to many past press releases in karate magazines, seldom fails to deter an attacker.

What exactly is kata, and is it the same for all styles of karate?

Kata is a series of prearranged offensive and defensive movements performed against imaginary opponents, much like shadowboxing. Different forms of kata are used in all styles of karate and formulate the basis for rank advancement in conjunction with other requirements, such as sparring ability and self-defense expertise. There are generally about twelve katas which have to be learned before advancing to the rank of black belt. Multiply this by the slightly less than a hundred various styles of karate, and it becomes apparent that there are literally thousands of variations. Very few are the same for all styles, although there do exist some distinct similarities. Many Japanese and Okinawan styles follow the patterns formulated by Gichin Funakoshi, the "father of modern karate." But even here there are small variations.

Was karate always called karate?

Karate (ka-*raw*-tay), meaning "empty-hand" or "China hand," depending on the translations of the Chinese ideogram, originated in Okinawa as te (*tay*) and was directly influenced by earlier Chinese martial arts. "Te" means "hand," and the Okinawans used such a misleading name because of the Japanese occupation, which would have put a stop to the practice. All weapons had been confiscated by the Japanese, and the ingenious Okinawan farmers developed and practiced te in secrecy. In a move toward nationalism, the Japanese later changed the name from "China hand" to mean "empty-hand."

Is it necessary to build calluses on the knuckles for karate?

This myth has been perpetuated by novitiates who didn't fully understand the purpose of the practice of hand conditioning. At one time hand and foot conditioning was considered a vital part of karate. But the practice has since been discontinued in the United States when it was learned that excessive hand conditioning could cause permanent damage and even paralysis. Forcibly striking or rubbing the hands and feet against a rough surface to toughen the skin and bone by building calluses and/or producing calcium deposits can lead to arthritis and rheumatism, it was discovered. One famous Japanese karate instructor who advocated the practice for many years now encounters throbbing pain when seated in an air-conditioned room, it's been reported.

Karate practitioners in the Orient still condition their hands and feet, however. Many possess enlarged knuckles, sometimes three or four times their normal size. They could walk on the grainiest concrete for miles without feeling any pain in their feet. The common doctrine behind skin and bone conditioning was that the practitioner could enhance his striking power and lessen the chance of damaging his own body when hitting an adversary.

Is karate really a form of self-defense?

Karate was formulated on the grounds of self-defense when Okinawan farmers, under pressure from the Japanese occupational forces several centuries ago, had to defend themselves against both weapons and empty-hand attacks. Almost every offensive move in karate has been developed as a counterattack against an opponent's initial technique. Even the kata, the formal exercises of karate performed like shadowboxing, begins and ends with a block, a direct reflection of the self-defense theory.

What is the correct term for what the layman refers to as the "chop"?

The chop is known as shuto (pronounced *shoo*-toe) in the Japanese vernacular. Literally translated, it means "knife hand," a strike with the fleshly, little-finger edge of the hand. It is nonetheless correct to call this technique a chop.

Is it beneficial to learn more than one style of karate?

There are two opinions. Open stylists believe a person can become more well-rounded if he learns techniques from several styles, though he should master the basics of one specific style first. In this way, a student could be capable of perfecting his hand techniques in, let's say, a Japanese system, and complementing his kicks by studying a Korean style.

The other school of thought derives from the traditionalists. They feel that practicing more than one style is a cardinal sin. In fact, if a student does so he may be asked to leave certain karate schools for good. The traditionalists believe it is a lifetime endeavor just to learn one system.

Roughly, how many 10th-degree karate black belts are living today?

Although the exact number is uncertain it is roughly estimated that there are at least two dozen who actually practice their arts today. Because it takes so many years to achieve this status and since most 10th-degree black belts are very advanced in age, many are retired and have passed the organizational duties on to their chief students. Most of these masters reside in Asia.

When a student executes a karate technique and his uniform snaps loudly, does that mean that he possesses extraordinary power?

Not necessarily. The way some karate uniforms are made today, a person could walk across the mat and the uniform would crackle. Many times, this deceiving crackling has promoted a false sense of security among beginners. This is not to say that the uniform shouldn't "pop" when a strong karate technique is delivered. However, the crisp popping sound is not an accurate method of gauging power.

In a real fighting situation, can kata be used?

Kata, the shadowboxing aspect of karate, cannot be used in actual combat in the same way that it is practiced in the dojo. That is, one cannot dance through a dozen movements when they are unnecessary to begin with. However, the individual self-defense movements can be extracted from the kata for fighting.

In a self-defense situation, should a beginner use karate?

In actual combat a beginner should use anything and everything he knows about fighting. He is cautioned not to use karate per se because of his inexperience with it. He would undoubtedly be sluggish and ineffective and would be biting off more than he can chew. Many times, too little experience is a dangerous commodity.

What is the highest degree one can achieve in karate?

The highest rank in karate is a 10th-degree black belt, usually attained only after an entire lifetime of study. Some karate systems, however, have rank only up to the 5th-degree black belt; some to 8th-degree.

What are the Golden Fist Awards?

Similar to Hollywood's Academy Awards, the Golden Fist Awards were founded in 1974 by Mike Stone for the purpose of honoring positive contributors to the growth of martial arts in Southern California. The first awards banquet cited individuals from Northern and Southern California alike. The second event, coproduced by Stuart Sobel and Creative Action, honored only those from Southern California. Recipients are judged in eight categories with special categories for those having achieved national prominence.

Why are stances important to karate?

Stances are very important to any martial art because foot positioning affects balance and the overall effectiveness of technique. Various stances in karate are utilized to promote balance, mobility, and/or stability for a compatible technique. For instance, many defensive techniques call for the use of a low, wide stance, while many offensive maneuvers are best launched from a high, narrow position of the feet to gain explosive acceleration.

Can one really toughen the hands by the consistent practice of penetrating containers of rice or beans?

Yes, but one can also permanently disfigure the hands by improperly applying these methods for extensive periods. The usual practice follows a logical progression from lighter materials to heavier. One generally starts out by stabbing his hands into a large container of rice a few times per day until his hands are toughened for coarser substances. He may then choose to use hard beans in place of rice, and then progress to sand. Consequently, the hands will become rough and callused. This is another form of hand conditioning, and the object is to strengthen striking power by possessing, in essence, a hand of iron.

Which is the most effective kata in karate?

Kata is only used in mock fighting situations with predetermined results. A real attack from an actual opponent doesn't occur. Therefore, all kata are effective for their overall goal or purpose, and none more so than any of the others. The common function is to teach the student rhythm, balance, speed, coordination, and basic techniques.

Why is karate called an art?

Karate, or any form of combat for that matter, can be considered an art when much of the emphasis is placed on form or correct body dynamics—aesthetic purposes rather than effectiveness or results. Much like ballet or ice skating, karate initially teaches a student to maneuver in an aesthetic manner. To make one's movements crisp and flawless requires perfect form. Thus, karate is a means of self-expression and a physical art form.

Are there any major styles of karate?

Yes. They are particularly apparent in the Japanese karate systems. The four major Japanese styles of karate are shotokan (*show*-toe-con), shito-ryu (*she*-toe-ryoo), wado-ryu (*waw*-doe-ryoo), and goju-ryu (*go*-jew-ryoo). The best-known Korean system is tae kwon do (tay-*quon*-doe). Okinawa has at least two very prominent styles in shorin-ryu (*shore*-in-ryoo) and isshin-ryu (*ish*-in-ryoo). But even here the large variation of styles becomes evident, as there are three styles of shorin-ryu karate alone. Kung-fu is divided into Northern and Southern Chinese systems with innumerable subdivisions.

Essentially, there are so many martial-arts systems that it has become increasingly difficult to determine which are major and which minor. Adding to the problem is the fact that each year the number of practitioners in each system increases and decreases dramatically. Some styles thus rise prominently as a major force one year, then drop to a minor style the next.

Do karate experts kick with their toes?

This is done very infrequently because of the possibility of injury. Probably because of the speed of a karate kick, many observers take it for granted that some strike with the toes. In reality, in a front kick, the toes are bent upward and the striking point is the ball of the foot. Some karate experts have developed such exceptional kicking speed that they do indeed break boards with the points of their toes upon occasion. However, it still is more practical to kick with other stronger areas of the foot, unless one is wearing shoes. Then, the point of the toe would be extremely efficient.

What is the Black Karate Federation?

The BKF, as it is better known, is an organization which was formed to solidify the black man's position in tournament karate by giving blacks a stronger voice in matters of judging and tournament policies. It also strongly promotes karate as a vehicle to keep black youths off the street and provide them with a movement with which to identify. Headquartered in Los Angeles, the unique association was founded by Steve Sanders, Jerry Smith, Ron Chapel, and Cliff Stewart. Though it is predominantly black, the federation is open to members of all races.

Who is the originator of "karate for Christ"?

Chattanooga's Mike Crain, an ordained minister, mixes martial arts and religion to spread the gospel. His "karate for Christ" campaign was reported in *Newsweek* several years ago, and Crain also appeared on a segment of the TV show *Thrillseekers.*

One of the most powerful karate techniques is the side thrust kick, as used here by Denver's Karyn Turner. Thrust and/or momentum techniques usually generate more power.

What is the most effective technique in karate?

The effectiveness of any karate technique can only be determined by several important factors: the situation in which it is used, the speed, rhythm, and power by which it is launched and landed, the target area on the opponent's body, and the opponent's position and his ability to absorb punishment. There are speed and there are power techniques employed in karate, but the effectiveness of either is dependent upon the aforementioned circumstances. Therefore, any single technique cannot be rightly called the *most* effective.

What are some of the more powerful karate techniques?

The reverse punch, the side kick, the spinning heel kick, and the ridge hand. These are generally thrust and/or momentum techniques and generate more power than snapping-type blows.

Have there ever been any deaths caused by karate?

There have been many rumors, but many times the actual death was caused by other sources, even when the victims were fighting in the karate ring. For instance, Santo Domingo's Victor Gloder died under mysterious circumstances twenty-six hours after leaving the scene of the 1975 Mexico vs. Dominican Republic Team Championships. Gloder had been close to being knocked down by Mexico's Ramiro Guzman in the second round, and, following the rest period, had entered the ring when he clutched his abdomen and doubled up in pain. The death was at first believed to have been from a blow he received in the ring. However, urine stains later discovered on the clothing of the deceased were tested and it was found that he had suffered from sickle-cell anemia. Doctors say the disease accounted for Gloder's untimely death. Other reported deaths in the martial arts have usually had similar causes; the victims were already suffering from a physical defect or disease.

How much power is generated by the karate punch?

The reverse punch, which travels in a straight line from the hip to its intended target, has never actually been gauged for power. However, there are certain physics principles which designate all karate movements. Besides its linear path, the reverse punch is delivered with the top two knuckles of the clenched fist. This physics principle can best be exemplified by the difference between the ball-peen hammer and a sledge hammer, or between casting a heavy stone and shooting a bullet. If you took a rock the size of your hand and hurled it against a wooden surface, it would probably cause a dent in the surface of the wood. On the other hand, if you shot a bullet into that same surface it would penetrate because of its speed. Therefore, it is taught in karate that maximum power can be obtained through speed instead of just mere mass. The speed principle applies to the reverse punch because it travels straight, with the line being the shortest distance between two points.

Why is the edge of the foot utilized in executing the side kick?

It is sharper than the flat foot and thus allows for greater shock when striking an opponent.

Why is the supporting knee bent when executing a kick with the opposite foot?

With the knee bent, there is greater balance maintained because the base foot isn't securely locked to the ground. Also, the hamstring muscles are relaxed with the knee bent, permitting greater kicking flexibility with the opposite leg.

Why does the elbow remain minutely bent when executing a karate punch?

First, fully extending one's elbow when executing a high-speed reverse punch can cause serious hyperextension to the elbow, since it will absorb shock generated by the punch, especially if the punch isn't landed against an opposing force. Other injuries, too, can result, such as water on the elbow (from continual practice of overextending the elbow) and the formation of calcium deposits at the elbow joint. By bending the elbow one generates maximum power without risking injury. Since most karate students practice by punching into the air and not against a surface, the risk of injury is greatly reduced.

Why do karate advocates lock their shoulders when punching?

Locking the shoulder causes the entire upper part of the body to be behind the punch, thus maximizing power. The erect shoulders also allow the karate practitioner to maintain balance in case an opponent evades the punch. Furthermore, the locked shoulders act as a brace, causing it to be more difficult for an opponent to pull one off balance.

Should the rear heel of the foot be on or off the ground when delivering a karate punch?

In traditional karate, the rear heel remains on the ground to reinforce the power generated by the punch. In sport karate, the heel is held off the ground when executing a punch because the emphasis is more on speed than power.

Why is the roundhouse kick a unique technique?

The roundhouse kick travels in a circular path parallel to the ground, with the knee acting as a gate upon which the bottom part of the leg swivels. The kick is unique because it can be brought around an opponent's extended hands to strike him in the head or in the body. Because it is deceiving, the roundhouse is the most often employed kick in sport karate.

Are circular karate techniques more effective than linear techniques?

It all depends on the situations in which each is employed. Circular techniques usually generate maximum force by using more parts of the body during the actual execution of the techniques. But if an opponent's defenses are set up accordingly, one would have to revert to linear patterns unless he instituted some type of faking action to change the opponent's position. Linear techniques employ the physics principle of taking the shortest distance between two points. Therefore, they require less body movement and can be executed in a shorter time. The proficient fighter learns to use circular and linear techniques alike in order to become unpredictable. Each type has its advantages and disadvantages.

When should one use linear techniques rather than circular techniques?

Linear techniques are generally used when one wants to attack quickly in the shortest possible time. Also, since linear techniques are mainly thrusting-type movements, they are stronger than some circular movements. Basically, when a great deal of power is required, linear techniques would be the logical choice.

Which style of karate is based on the "hard-soft" principle of motion?

The literal translation of the goju-ryu (*go*-jew-ryoo) style of karate is "hard-soft way." The system combines elements of both hard and soft movements or linear and circular techniques.

Do children learn full-contact when they are enrolled in a karate school?

Absolutely not. Children are taught self-defense first before even moving into light, noncontact sparring. American karate instructors are very conscientious about teaching children under the safest possible conditions, since injuries incurred at a young age can often become permanent afflictions. Therefore, youngsters are held in high regard and every measure is taken to safeguard their health. If an inexperienced karate instructor is teaching your child full-contact sport karate, it is recommended that you place him under the guidance of a more conscientious teacher in another school.

Are adults required to learn full-contact when enrolling in a karate school?

No. Adults enroll for various reasons: physical fitness, self-defense, philosophy, or mental stimulation. Very few are interested in or made to compete in full-contact contests. An adult should reveal his reasons for taking up karate to the instructor when he or she first signs up for lessons.

What type of karate lessons should an adult have when he or she enrolls in a school?

The lessons should be geared to the individual; the individual shouldn't be geared to the lessons, because every person is skilled and motivated differently. Sometimes it is difficult to obtain maximum individual results in a classroom situation. This is why nearly every professional instructor will also offer private lessons to his students. Private lessons are more expensive, but unbeatable for obtaining maximum individual improvement. An adult must always keep in mind that if a karate school offers "professional" services, that does not necessarily mean "professional" full-contact karate services. It merely means that a karate instructor is most probably conducting his school professionally as a business. A professional can usually offer more benefits to students than can a part-time instructor who makes his living from a profession outside the martial arts.

Which karate association was the first to organize in the United States?

According to Robert Trias of Phoenix, Arizona, he formed the United States Karate Association (USKA) in 1948 with Atlee Cheetham of Texas as his first affiliate. Membership in the then new association fluctuated between thirteen and twenty for the first several years. Currently, the USKA stands out as one of the largest karate bodies in America, and its membership includes karate practitioners of all styles from across the continent.

What was one of the most impressive karate demonstrations ever staged?

Indisputably, one would have to be the public karate exhibitions used by

Robert Trias (right), founder of the United States Karate Association, shaking hands with USKA Grand National champion Flem Evans. Looking on is Parker Shelton.

Japan's Mas Oyama to battle bulls. In his lifetime Oyama has pitted his unusual strength and karate skills against fifty-two of the huge beasts. He severed the horns from forty-eight of them, and he killed three others who were marked for slaughter. Through these demonstrations Oyama convinced even the most skeptical observers that karate was a highly effective means of combat.

Are there major styles of Korean karate other than tae kwon do?

Yes. Much as in the Chinese, Okinawan, and Japanese martial arts, there are a great many subdivisions. Some of the lesser-known Korean systems are chang mu kwan, chi do kwan, chung do kwan, han mu kwan, hapkido, hwarang-do, jee do kwan, kwonpup or kwon bop, mu duk kwan, oh do kwan, sang mu kwan, subak, tae kwon (early tae kwon do) and tang soo do.

Are there any karate styles which originated in Hawaii?

There are two major combative disciplines which find their roots in the Pineapple State, but they aren't necessarily referred to as karate. Probably the better-known art is kenpo, the style Ed Parker introduced to the continental United States in 1954. Kenpo, or "fist law," as defined by Parker is a "modern term describing one of the more innovative systems practiced in Hawaii and the Americas. Kenpo employs linear as well as circular moves, utilizing intermittent power when and where needed, interspersed with minor and major moves which flow with continuity. It is flexible in thought and action so as to blend with encounters as they occur."

The other major Hawaiian style is kajukenbo (ka-jew-*ken*-bow). Kajukenbo contains both hard and soft movements and was conceived in Hawaii in 1947 by five practitioners: Walter Choo (karate), Joseph Holke (judo), Frank Ordonez (jujutsu), Adriano Emperado (kenpo), and Clarence Chang (Chinese boxing). The name "kajukenbo" was contractionally derived from the styles of its founders: *ka* is from karate, *ju* from judo and jujutsu, *ken* from kenpo, and *bo* from Chinese boxing.

What is the Okinawan karate salutation?

The Okinawan salutation is performed with one outstretched hand covering the clenched fist, and begins at chin level and traverses down to the belt level. At all times, the knuckles of the clenched fist are covered. Otherwise, it symbolizes a challenge to the person being faced, perhaps an instructor who is teaching or overseeing the form one is about to do immediately following the salutation. Besides being grounds for a duel, the exposed knuckles are also a sign of disrespect.

What is the Tracy System?

The Tracy System is a combination of martial arts, business, and salesmanship provided for franchisees of the Tracy's chain of karate schools. Tracy's became the foremost chain-school operation in American karate during the late 1960s and early 1970s. The chain's founders, Jim and Al Tracy, are brothers who created the enterprise shortly after gaining their initial karate training with California karate pioneer Ed Parker.

Which style of karate is the most prevalent in the United States?

Either the Japanese shotokan or the Korean tae kwon do styles. There have been no real statistics to gauge the growth of these two popular systems, but the great influx of Oriental instructors of these disciplines to the United States points to them as the two most widely taught.

How did karate spread from Japan to the United States?

Most noticeably, through servicemen who studied in the Orient and returned to America to open karate schools of their own.

What was the feat performed in order to get karate into the *Guinness Book of World Records?*

A group of four British karate practitioners smashed two thousand roofing tiles in three minutes, thirty-three seconds, and ultimately the feat was included in the famous journal. The feat was performed in London by Phil Milner, Edgar Oakland, Jack Holt, and Martin Dixon.

Why should toenails and fingernails be clipped during karate practice?

Principally to avoid injury. When sparring, even on a friendly basis, a long nail can easily find its way into an opponent's eye or other tender areas. Most women, however, do not practice much sparring and instead participate more in self-defense training. Many coaches thus allow them to keep their nails long.

Why is jewelry usually not worn by karate competitors?

Obviously, rings, watches and other adornments can cause serious injury to an opponent. Even when performing kata, the shadowboxing aspect of karate not requiring a partner, jewelry can inflict injuries on the person wearing it.

Was karate taught to the Armed Forces during World War II?

No. The Armed Forces at that time were only taught a crash course in hand-to-hand combat. Before the war, there was perhaps no one in the United States with a knowledge of karate.

How much should karate lessons cost?

On an average, most facilities charge merely $25 to $30 per month. This will usually entitle the student to use of the facilities for as many as six days per week, and one evening group class. There are numerous variations which reflect on payment rates, such as the number of students enrolling simultaneously, and the amount of down payment one applies to the overall fee. Many schools feature a two-for-the-price-of-one rate. Others have a family rate. The best method of determining the prices at schools in your community is to shop around. Select the dojo, or school, that best accommodates your time schedule and budget.

What standard equipment should a dojo have?

All well-equipped dojos should have mirrors, punching bags, preferably a matted or padded floor, some sort of movable, light bag for accuracy training, a stretch bar, and, if possible, protective hand and foot gear to practice full-focused blows. The construction of many facilities in some states doesn't allow for padding or matting on the floor. This is more common on the West Coast.

What is a makiwara board?

The makiwara (maw-key-*war*-a) is a straw-padded striking post designed to be forcibly struck for toughening various striking points on the anatomy. It is either secured firmly to the ground on a wooden post, or hung against the dojo wall. In the early days of karate in America, hours of training were spent hitting the makiwara in order to build calluses on the knuckles and the feet. However, because its overuse can cause possible permanent damage, the makiwara is now used only on occasion. It is an excellent training aid for developing and focusing strength for techniques.

Are there karate schools with just female members?

There are four widely known exclusively female karate schools in the United States. The oldest and most successful is Karate for Women, established in Portland, Oregon, by Pauline Short in 1965. Short left a well-paying job as a graphic artist to open her school more than a decade ago. It started in the basement of a Buddhist church and today boasts an enrollment of two hundred women, many of whom have engaged in the sporting aspect of karate rather than merely in self-defense training.

Two more such facilities, in Seattle, Washington, are owned by Py Bateman. Head of the Feminist Karate Union, Bateman opened her first school in 1971. From its original fifteen students it grew rapidly in size and since 1973 has maintained an enrollment of between one hundred and two hundred students. Her second studio, located in West Seattle, opened in the fall of 1973. The FKU is operated as a corporation in which Bateman, as president, is subject to direction by a board of directors elected from among the schools' students.

Mikie Rowe operates an all-women's dojo in Richmond, California, in conjunction with a figure salon. She maintains about forty students. It has also been reported that there are several exclusively female schools in and around New York City. For information, one can write to the Women's Martial Arts Union, P.O. Box 1463, New York, N.Y. 10027 or call (212)233–5949.

How can you tell whether or not a karate instructor is legitimate?

These days, rank certificates, which formerly attested to the validity of an instructor, have become a very controversial issue. Black-belt diplomas can be obtained just about anywhere, and no stringent guidelines exist to measure the recipient's ability. Since there are no regulated quality controls in karate, the best method of determining whether or not an instructor is legitimate is to ask an established martial-arts publication. Since this method will take approximately three months before you'll receive a reply, there is an alternative other than just calling a magazine. Observe several classes at the school at which you are interested in enrolling. Talk to the students and instructor, check the Better Business Bureau in case there have been complaints, and determine how long the school has been in operation.

Which part of the body is most important to karate?

The hands, because they can be used both offensively and defensively.

How close does one come when pulling a punch or a kick in karate?

For noncontact tournament competition a scoring technique has to come within one inch of the intended target on the opponent's body, and it has to be executed with maximum power. However, in both public and private demonstrations of this nature, black belts have been able to pull full-force blows within fractions of an inch of a partner. In regular dojo practice, blows are pulled close enough to demonstrate to students that they can be landed if necessary.

Can a person who wears glasses study karate?

Yes. A sight defect is not detrimental to one's ability to learn any martial art. If your vision is extremely poor it is strongly recommended that you don't take off the glasses, especially when sparring.

Is karate still evolving, or has it reached its final form?

Some practitioners contend that with the introduction of full-contact karate competition it has reached its final stage of development. Ironically, karate was originally created centuries ago as a means of unarmed warfare when the Okinawan people were repressed by the occupying Japanese military forces. It was then full-contact in its most deadly form—that is, with the outcome meaning the difference between life and death. However, reflecting on the history of karate and its many variations and methods of practice, one can only surmise that it will evolve infinitely. That is perhaps why it can never be considered a stale art or athletic form.

Are karate's flying kicks effective?

According to a poll taken by *Karate Illustrated Magazine* several years ago, 64 percent of the experienced black belts interviewed supported the contention that kicks launched in the air were devastating. Twenty-four percent claimed they weren't as effective as techniques launched from a position on the ground; 12 percent wanted to know the specific situation in which such kicks would be used before they would voice an opinion.

Is karate suffering from commercialism?

There are two points of view. From the viewpoint of those groups and individuals concerned with progress, karate has made great inroads by spreading worldwide and offering the average person an athletic activity, a means of self-protection, and a unique method of physical conditioning. On the other hand, purists feel that commercialism has diluted the original mental and spiritual values inherent to karate. This difference has brought about two major factions in the karate industry, commonly referred to as the traditionalists and the commercialists.

What is the world's largest karate association?

According to statistics claimed by the World Tae Kwon Do Association, it is the largest organization in the world today. The president, General Choi Hong Hi, claims to have millions of members worldwide in the organization.

How is a karate rank examination given?

Examinations are generally held in four stages, depending on the rank level for which a student is being tested. The first part usually consists of a demonstration of basics—stances, punches, strikes, kicks, blocks, and combinations of these basics. In the second stage, the candidate is graded on his or her performance of kata or form, which generally consists of numerous forms of various degrees of difficulty, and in some instances, a kata of the student's personal choice. Thirdly, an exhibition of the candidate's free-sparring ability is required, sometimes against more than one opponent. Finally, the student is quizzed on his knowledge regarding origin, history, and technicalities of the martial arts.

Sport Karate

When Gichin Funakoshi, the "father of modern karate," devised a method of safely practicing karate without injury to its participants, he undoubtedly failed to foresee the proportions to which his innovation would expand. Funakoshi called it free-sparring, which permitted two students to engage in a karate match without actually making contact with the hands and feet. In 1952, Funakoshi's celebrated student Tsutomu Ohshima, later to become the "father of Shotokan karate in America," invented an organized system of conducting karate matches complete with judges and scoring procedures. Eleven years later, on July 28, 1963, Arizona's Robert Trias staged the first "national" karate tournament on American soil at the University of Chicago Fieldhouse. It is probable that even Ohshima and Trias had no idea how popular their particular activities would become.

Today, sport karate has been divided into three distinct phases: noncontact for amateurs, semi-contact for aspiring professionals, and full-contact for only the most intrepid karate warrior. Combined, the sport now has thousands of enthusiasts who ply their skills in hundreds of tournaments throughout every continent in the world. The innovations have been many, the variations extreme. But in view of the progress made in America, it should be only a short time before the sport—at least the full-contact phase—becomes a major national attraction for the general public.

Because of the ever-increasing interest, it is perhaps surprising that no one has taken a stab at compiling an adequate record book. What unfolds on the following pages, however, is the most accurate and comprehensive information ever presented publicly. The data should help the reader understand the many transformations the sport has endured and the heights it has reached on its way to achieving international popularity.

Who has won more full-contact bouts than any other fighter to date?

California's Benny "The Jet" Urquidez holds a win-loss record of 29–0 at the time of this writing. Twenty-six of his fights were won by knockout.

Who was the leading money-winner in full-contact karate competition for 1975?

Benny Urquidez earned more than $30,000 in prize money for 1975.

What is the highest-paid live gate for a martial-arts event?

The 1974 Oriental World of Self-Defense at Madison Square Garden attracted 19,564 spectators, according to promoter Aaron Banks, for an entire program of martial-arts demonstrations mixed with circus-type displays. The paid live gate reached $100,000.

Which karate tournament has drawn the largest number of competitors?

The 1974 International Karate Championships in Long Beach, California, drew nearly six thousand contestants, according to figures provided by promoter Ed Parker.

What role has kick-boxing played in the formulation of sport karate?

Kick-boxing took hold in American sport karate in 1969, shortly after the first wave of professional karate tournaments. Only a handful of bouts took place, however, in the more densely populated areas such as Los Angeles, Dallas, and New York City. The so-called kick-boxers were converted karate fighters with a yen for full-contact fighting. Kick-boxing experienced a sudden and rapid death simultaneously with professional karate in 1970. However, professional karate fighting made its successful comeback in 1973, while kick-boxing did not. Lee Faulkner, a California promoter, introduced local televised kick-boxing matches in Los Angeles in 1971. The matches were conducted between actual Thailand kick-boxers and enjoyed moderate popularity in the area. One year later, the California State Athletic Commission, which regulates all boxing and wrestling exhibitions and contests, altered its existing rules to include kick-boxing, and, for reasons undisclosed, the weekly kick-boxing telecasts were discontinued soon afterward.

Who was the first big money-winner in professional karate?

Howard Jackson, nicknamed "The California Flash" for his explosive fighting style in semi-contact professional karate, was the first prominent money-winner in 1973, when the professional aspect of the sport was restored. From July to December, Jackson won $2,500. His earnings were considered large, because it was the real beginning of established professional karate.

What is the difference between noncontact and semi-contact karate?

Noncontact sport karate can be more appropriately called light-contact, because light to moderate contact to the body is permitted, according to standard rules. In all cases of noncontact and light-contact competition, excessive face contact is grounds for immediate disqualification. In semi-contact karate, fighters don protective equipment and are permitted to land blows to both the head and body with controlled, restrained force. Semi-contact is considered the stepping stone to full-contact professional karate. Noncontact is principally fought by the sport's amateurs.

Tournament karate titles have been deceiving. Which are the real "national" karate tourneys?

Because there is no single authoritative body governing sport karate elimination events, national tournaments, where titles are significant, have largely been decided by the individual tourney's ability to draw top-caliber fighters from all over the country. Since the early 1970s, the most important annual elimination tournaments have been the Battle of Atlanta, held by Joe Corley in Georgia; Robert Trias' USKA Grand Nationals, in which the location alternates between the Midwest and the Southeast; Ed Parker's International Karate Championships in Long Beach, California; Mike Anderson's Top 10 Nationals, usually staged in St. Louis, Missouri; and Allen Steen's U.S. Championships in Dallas, Texas. These annual events have withstood the test of time and continually draw the nation's better fighters.

In full-contact sport karate there are several organizations which sponsor and sanction major closed-card events. Their set-up is similar to the National Football League or baseball's American League. The most notable of these organizations are Jhoon Rhee's World Blackbelt League, a team concept headquartered in Washington, D.C.; the Professional Karate Association (PKA), run by Don and Judy Quine of Hollywood; the World Martial Arts Council, operated by Mike Anderson out of Oklahoma City; and Aaron Banks's World Professional Karate Organization, headquartered in New York City.

World lightweight champion Benny Urquidez scoring a clean point on former Top 10– ▶ ranked John Natividad. As in all noncontact karate matches, blows to the face are pulled just short of contact.

What is the highest paid gate for a karate tournament?

Mike Anderson, in conjunction with Don and Judy Quine of the Professional Karate Association, grossed $50,000 at the innovative World Professional Karate Championships at the Los Angeles Sports Arena in September 1974.

What is the "Johnson" ruling and how did it influence sport karate?

In 1968, veteran referee Pat Johnson of California originated the "penalty point" system for excessive contact. Years before karate reached its current full-contact stage, the "Johnson" ruling, as it came to be known, ended the uncontrolled blood-and-guts era of so-called noncontact sport karate. Johnson's conscientious innovation, introduced at the National Black Belt Championships in Albuquerque, New Mexico, and still in use today in amateur competition, was to save many a fighter from broken bones and chipped teeth.

Under the rule, competitors who make excessive contact give away one point to their opponents. Prior to the ruling, if a fighter was struck so hard that he couldn't continue he was penalized by disqualification.

Which elimination karate tournament has run consistently for the longest period of time?

The United States Karate Association (USKA) Grand Nationals began in 1963 as the World Karate Championships. Although it has twice changed titles since then, it has operated annually since its inception and is the longest-running national karate tourney in America.

Have there been any bare-knuckle full-contact karate tournaments?

Unfortunately, yes, even though they violate federal law. In 1967, the late John Keehan, better known as Count Dante, staged a bare-knuckle, fight-to-the-finish brawl under the sanction of the World Fighting Arts Federation, his personal association. Dubbing it a "World Championships," his announcement to the martial-arts community aroused severe criticism when it was discovered he intended to have contestants engage in bare-knuckle, full-contact matches. Disapproval was so general that no one but his own students competed in Keehan's event. His student Vic Ryther won first-place honors. Years later, Ryther told prominent karate sportswriter Massad Ayoob, "There were eight contestants. One quit. No one was injured. It was completely no-holds-barred. There was supposed to be $10,000 [in prize money], and it was supposed to be backed by Chicago wrestling, then it came down to a hundred bucks or something like that."

In early 1975, New York's Fred Hamilton staged a bare-knuckle, full-contact tournament. The turnout was sparse and the martial-arts media summed it up as a disaster, both in participant turnout and at the box office.

What was the first major karate tournament ever to be nationally televised?

In 1965, ABC's *Wide World of Sports* televised Jhoon Rhee's National Karate Championships out of Washington, D.C. Because of a heated match between grand champion Mike Stone and runner-up Walt Worthy, *Wide World* execs were less than pleased with the results. Nine years later, they returned to televise Allen Steen's U.S. Championships in Dallas. Ironically enough, Mike Stone was responsible for persuading them to film the event.

Who were the two most underrated fighters of the 1960s?

Kansan Jim Harrison and Californian Bob Wall. Harrison, a rough-and-tumble mauler, was never rated in Top 10 polls or received adequate press coverage from the existing martial-arts media during his heyday. And yet, furious battles in which things like broken bones didn't stop him from winning are now a matter of legend.

Bob Wall consistently placed second and third in every major U.S. karate tournament from 1965–71, many times bowing out to his instructor, the legendary Joe Lewis. Also overlooked by the martial-arts printed media, and falling in the shadow of his teacher, Wall was thus unheralded as a fighter of national caliber. He received his most significant endorsement in 1970, however, when he was selected as the fifth member of the World Professional Karate Team Champions by its other distinguished members—Lewis, Chuck Norris, Mike Stone, and Skipper Mullins.

What is the largest sum of prize money ever awarded at a pro/am karate tournament?

Ed Parker gave away $16,250 at his 1975 International Karate Championships in Long Beach, California.

What is the largest sum of prize money ever promised but not delivered at a pro/am karate tournament?

Prize money at Eugene Forte's Pro/Am World Association of Karate (PAWAK) Championships in May 1974 amounted to $40,000. Heavyweight Joe

Lewis won first place and was supposed to be paid $10,000 cash and a Mark IV Lincoln. However, promoter Forte, who had never previously been involved in karate, awarded postdated checks in place of the expected cash settlements. Seventeen days later all the checks bounced. Following a court settlement one year later with a Los Angeles insurance firm with which Forte had posted a bond to guarantee the prize money, Lewis received about $8,000. All other winners were forced to settle for approximately 80 percent of their original awards. Lewis never got the Mark IV. It had been driven back to the car lot by the salesman on the evening of the tourney because Forte had failed to pay the required cash for the car. The car-lot owner just wouldn't accept a check.

What is the largest sum of prize money ever awarded at a full-contact karate event?

In September 1974, promoter Mike Anderson awarded $20,000 in total prize money to four full-contact champions in four respective weight divisions at his historic World Professional Karate Championships. Each champion received $3,000, and runners-up also were awarded a lesser share of the overall stakes.

Where does the United States rank in relation to other countries in sport-karate competition?

America, because of its sudden explosion in karate popularity and its increased tournament activity, is considered the stronghold of competitive play. In major open professional competition, Americans have consistently dominated players from other nations except in a few rare cases of noncontact bouts. The Japanese have, however, reigned supreme in the international amateur competitions organized by the World Union of Karate-Do Organizations (WUKO). Since WUKO has endorsed the AAU (Amateur Athletic Union) as the sole representative of U.S. amateur karate, there has been merely one large international event staged. American fighters failed to place in either individual or team contests, even though it was held on their own home turf. America has been poorly represented in these organized amateur events since the high-caliber fighters pursue the professional aspects of sport karate. In international professional karate, the United States has never failed to win unanimous victories.

What is the Battle of Atlanta?

Created by Joe Corley in 1970, the annual Battle of Atlanta is one of the largest and most prestigious karate elimination tournaments in the United States. It was the scene of the first defense of a world title in professional full-contact karate in 1975 when Corley squared off against world middleweight champion Bill Wallace

Joe Corley, founder of the annual Battle of Atlanta, prepares for his historic full-contact match with world middleweight champion Bill Wallace.

of Memphis in nine two-minute rounds of furious action. The regulation semi-contact part of the event has been a major attraction for aspiring fighters since 1973.

Who was the first authentic "national" karate champion?

AlGene Caraulia of Cleveland, Ohio, became the sport's first champion when he won top honors in the World Karate Championships at the Chicago Coliseum in 1963. It was the first tournament in America to draw top karate fighters of the period from all parts of the nation.

Who compiled the most impressive tournament record during the 1960s?

California's Mike Stone (now of Las Vegas, Nevada) claims to have gone undefeated in eighty-nine black belt matches. But karate has been plagued by inadequate recordkeeping, which caused some skeptics to dispute whether or not Stone was actually defeated at some point in his fighting career. His critics claim he lost an unpublicized match in Texas, but there exists no proof to substantiate the claim.

Who are considered the greatest fighters in sport karate?

In the noncontact era of the 1960s, four fighters were looked upon as the greatest champions of the period. Mike Stone, Chuck Norris, and Joe Lewis, all of Southern California, and Skipper Mullins of Texas scored unprecedented competitive records. In 1973–74, when the sport moved into its semi-contact stage, lightweight Howard Jackson of Los Angeles emerged as the sport's most distinguished fighter.

In September 1974, concurrent with sport karate's move into full-contact fighting, at least three of four champions crowned at Mike Anderson's World Professional Karate Championships were considered the greatest fighters of the new era. Middleweight Bill Wallace of Memphis, lightheavyweight Jeff Smith of Washington, D.C., and heavyweight veteran Joe Lewis of Hollywood established their full-contact titles at the event. Although Mexico's Isaias Duenas was the Professional Karate Association's original world lightweight champion, he has been replaced by Benny Urquidez of San Fernando, California.

Which full-contact karate match is considered the most exciting to date?

There are two opinions. The nine-round bout between Bill Wallace and Joe Corley at the 1975 Battle of Atlanta is generally viewed as the most exciting fight in the history of the sport. It was Wallace's first successful title defense of his world middleweight crown. On the other hand, some observers feel the eleven-round match between world lightheavyweight champion Jeff Smith of Washington, D.C., and New Jersey's Karriem Allah was equally exciting. The match played before 50 million spectators worldwide on the Ali/Frazier "Thrilla in Manila" card. Smith won a split decision.

At the Deutschlandhalle Arena in West Berlin, Germany, Gordon Franks (right) won a nine-round decision over Mexico's Ramiro Guzman to become karate's first world super-lightweight titlist.

Where did Gordon Franks win his world title?

St. Paul's Gordon Franks, the world superlightweight champion of full-contact karate, earned his title in West Berlin, Germany, at the Deutschlandhalle Arena in 1975. Franks won a nine-round decision over Mexico City's Ramiro Guzman. The fight recorded several firsts in the history of karate competition. It was the first world-title fight staged outside of the United States, and Franks is the first champion established in the superlightweight division.

Franks has yet to receive the acclaim of his karate world champion counterparts in other divisions, perhaps because he has not been as active. Ideally, though, Franks represents the "new" kind of professional karate athlete—handsome, intelligent, and articulate, with three years of college education behind him.

Along with his coaches, John and Pat Worley, Franks teaches karate at the Jhoon Rhee Institute in Bloomington, Minnesota.

Which American fighter was the most famous kick-boxer?

In kick-boxing within the United States, karate fighter Joe Lewis gained the most formidable reputation. He successfully defended his title ten times before U.S. kick-boxing died out in 1970. Before that, Lewis was one of the most consistent noncontact champions on the karate circuit.

Who is Europe's most distinguished karate fighter?

Dominic Valera of Paris, France, has won 587 out of 602 official noncontact matches since he started competing in 1966. Some of these matches were won in minor U.S. karate tournaments.

What is the largest sum of prize money ever won by a single karate fighter?

Legendary Joe Lewis was promised $10,000 for winning first place in the Pro/Am World Association of Karate Championships in Long Beach, California, in May 1974. At least that was the figure which appeared on the postdated check he received in place of the promised cash. He also was to receive a Mark IV Lincoln, which was never delivered. Following a court settlement one year later, Lewis collected nearly $8,000 from the promoter's insurance company. The sum still stands as the largest sum awarded to a karate fighter. An interesting point is that the fighters engaged in noncontact fighting, and, to date, no full-contact champion has received as much for a single performance.

How would a karate or kung-fu fighter fare against a boxer?

If a martial artist was limited to participate under boxing rules where he could only use his gloved hands instead of kicking, sweeping, and takedowns, he would probably lose such an encounter, depending upon his individual ability. These types of bouts have frequently taken place under a variety of rules with a variety of contrasting results. In the final analysis, again, the outcome depends largely on the capabilities of the individuals engaging in such contests, regardless of which combative discipline is used.

Is karate truly an international sport?

Yes. There have already been two significant professional events in Germany where America's top fighters competed against Europeans. In the amateur ranks, three world championships have been presented in Japan, Paris, and America, where as many as thirty-eight various nations have participated.

Why do karate fighters bow to one another before and after a match?

Bowing is a customary gesture of respect for each other's abilities. It is a part of Japanese culture introduced simultaneously with karate. Contestants also bow to the referee at the beginning and end of each match.

What was the first open karate tournament staged in America?

The North American Karate Championships held at Madison Square Garden in New York City in 1962.

Who won the first open karate tournament in the United States?

New Jersey's Gary Alexander, who has since retired.

Which full-contact karate match was considered the most important to date?

Perhaps the Jeff Smith/Karriem Allah match, because it was seen by 50 million viewers worldwide on television and closed-circuit TV as a preliminary bout to the classic Ali/Frazier match on the "Thrilla in Manila" card. It by far outdistanced any previous karate broadcast.

Is there prize money awarded in kata competition?

Yes. Mike Anderson started professional kata (form) competition at his 1974 Top 10 Nationals in St. Louis, Missouri, by awarding $500 to the first- through fourth-place winners. The innovation took off in 1975 when Anderson's brainchild, *Professional Karate Magazine,* began regularly rating the Top 10 kata competitors in America for the first time. Also in 1975, the nation's major karate elimination tournaments adopted the concept. Joe Corley's Battle of Atlanta, Robert Trias' USKA Grand Nationals, Ed Parker's Internationals, and Anderson's Top 10 Nationals all awarded prize money to form contestants. Parker gave an unprecedented $1,000.

What are some of Chuck Norris' major victories?

During the 1960s, Chuck Norris stood out as one of the big three all-time champions, along with Joe Lewis and Mike Stone, who individually won every major title in their sport. Norris won grand championship titles at the '67 and '68 All American Open in New York; the '68 National Karate Championships in Washington, D.C.; the '67 and '68 International Karate Championships in Long Beach, California; the '68 and '69 World Professional Karate Championships in New York City; and the middleweight title of the U.S. Championships in Dallas, Texas. In addition, he won dozens of minor titles. Norris' middleweight throne has been taken over by Bill Wallace.

World heavyweight champion Joe Lewis (left) on the way to winning the grand championship title of the USKA Grand Nationals.

What are some of Joe Lewis' major tournament victories?

As a fledgling black belt, Joe Lewis entered his first karate tournament in 1966, the National Karate Championships in Washington, D.C., promoted by Jhoon Rhee. He stunned competitors and observers alike by sweeping the grand championship his first time out against such favored contenders as New York's Thomas LaPuppet. His feat was akin to an amateur golfer winning the U.S. Pro/Am his first time out. Lewis' overall competitive record accounts for more than thirty major titles, a record still unequaled in the annals of sport karate. He was the only four-time winner of the National Karate Championships and three-time winner of the International Karate Championships in Long Beach in sport karate history. In 1970, Lewis became the U.S. Heavyweight Kick-boxing Champion, and he went on to defend his title ten times with no opponent lasting through the second round. After retiring from 1972–74, he returned to win the heavyweight title of Mike Anderson's and the PKA's World Professional Karate Championships in Los Angeles. Lewis later lost two unofficial full-contact matches to Hawaii's Teddy Limoz and Indiana's Ross Scott, but retired officially in late 1975 as the world heavyweight karate champion.

Why is Mike Stone considered a legend in his own time?

The accounts of Mike Stone's powerful fighting style and his impressive tournament record have made him a legend in his own time. Stone achieved the rank of black belt in merely six months. He then initiated his extraordinary competitive career in 1963, and before retiring in 1969, he claims to have compiled an undefeated record of eighty-nine wins and no losses as a black belt. He lost two early matches as a brown belt, and was only forced into an overtime situation once in Chicago, when fighting a Japanese player named Yogi. Stone is considered the retired world professional lightheavyweight champion, and his throne has been justifiably occupied by Jeff Smith.

Whatever happened to Skipper Mullins?

Considered the premier lightweight champion of the 1960s, Skipper Mullins is still active in teaching karate in Dallas. From 1964 to '68, Mullins won first place in every division from white through black belt at the prestigious International Karate Championships. Before retiring in 1972, he also won lightweight and middleweight titles at the '67, '71, and '72 All American Open in Oklahoma; he was the '67 Top 10 champion, and the '68 to '71 world professional lightweight champion. At one point in his career, from May 1966 to February 1967, he fought in forty-two tournaments. On one weekend in February '67, Mullins fought in New York City on Friday; Dallas, Texas, on Saturday; and Los Angeles on Sunday. He won two of these three events. In six of the seven years he competed as a black belt, Mullins was ranked among the Top 10 fighters in America by *Black Belt Magazine.* He retired as the undefeated world professional lightweight champion. The most clear-cut successor to his vacant throne has been California's Benny "The Jet" Urquidez.

Was there ever a World Professional Karate Team?

Yes, although it has been rather overlooked as a major incident in American sport karate. Perhaps this is due to the fact that the team members have all retired and have never had to defend the title following their initial victory. The World Professional Team Championships was conceived by Southern California promoter Lee Faulkner. He held the prestigious event at the Long Beach Arena in 1970. Faulkner gathered together for the first time sport karate's greatest fighters of the period to form one team. Serving on that historic contingent were Mike Stone, Joe Lewis, Chuck Norris, and Skipper Mullins. They voted to accept Bob Wall unanimously as the fifth member of the team. The contingent handily defeated all comers to run away with the crown.

What is Ron Marchini's claim to fame?

Ron was twice ranked the number-one noncontact fighter in United States karate by *Black Belt Magazine.* He is one of the premier tournament fighters of the 1960s, and he maintained an impressive competitive record during the early '70s. Marchini, in addition to operating a chain of karate studios in and around Stockton, California, has starred in and produced motion pictures.

Who are the most prominent full-contact coaches?

The undisputed major advocate of full-contact karate fighting has been Joe Lewis, who trained under full-contact conditions as far back as 1966, when noncontact tournaments were the only existing type of karate competition. Lewis' protégé Jerry Smith, along with Arnold Urquidez and Jhoon Rhee of Washington, D.C., are perhaps the most prominent full-contact karate coaches in contemporary karate.

Which is the most famous full-contact tournament?

Mike Anderson, in conjunction with Don and Judy Quine and the Professional Karate Association, held the innovative World Professional Karate Champion-

Members of the first World Professional Karate Team (left to right) are Bob Wall, Chuck Norris, Skipper Mullins, Mike Stone, and in sweat suit, Joe Lewis. To Lewis' left is promoter Lee Faulkner.

ships at the Los Angeles Sports Arena on September 14, 1974. The novel event revolutionized sport karate by kicking off the current emphasis on full-contact competition. It featured fourteen fighters from seven countries throughout the world. The United States was represented by the undisputed best fighters in the nation—Howard Jackson, Jeff Smith, Bill Wallace, and Joe Lewis. Anderson awarded an unprecedented $20,000 in total prize money. The event was later shown twice on ABC's *Wide World of Entertainment,* the first time receiving the highest rating for a *Wide World* special in 1974.

Who is the best-known American to promote karate on the East Coast?

Aaron Banks of New York stands out as the most prolific American entrepreneur

America's most prolific karate promoter, New York's Aaron Banks, has presented more than 150 martial-arts events. Also a black belt, here he executes a side kick.

on the East Coast. Though he often substitutes quantity for quality, the veteran's record of staging more than a hundred various karate events is unprecedented by any other promoter in the entire United States. Banks has presented countless innovative events, including his highly successful Oriental World of Self-Defense, which brought in the first $100,000 paid gate; the East Coast vs. West Coast Team Championships; the second World Professional Karate Championships, back in '68, when he gathered the era's best noncontact fighters; and his promoting of the Gogen "The Cat" Yamaguchi exposition.

Who was the Frank Ruiz protégé who became a nationally ranked fighter?

Louis Delgado, a Ruiz student, was a four-time member of *Black Belt Mag-*

azine's Top 10 fighters from 1968 to 1971. Delgado later moved to Los Angeles, where he studied with the late Bruce Lee, Chuck Norris, Bob Wall, and Pat Johnson.

Which American female has attained the greatest prominence in sport karate?

Denver's Malia Dacascos, a highly proficient kung-fu exponent, gained national acclaim during the 1970s for consistently defeating men in kata, or form, competition. Also ranked the number-one female fighter by *Professional Karate Magazine*, Dacascos became the only woman to be rated in the 1975 national Top 10 form ratings in the United States. She has now unofficially retired, but gives frequent demonstrations of her art along with her husband, Al Dacascos, a retired national fighting and form champion.

Which husband-and-wife team are known as the king and queen of American kung-fu?

The martial-arts media bestowed the title on Al and Malia Dacascos of Denver, Colorado. The duo became one of the most prominent man-and-wife teams in sport karate history when they began winning championship titles in major events across the country. They were the first kung-fu advocates to actively and successfully compete in the sport.

For what innovation is Soloman Kaihewalu credited?

Kaihewalu has demonstrated a knack for innovative karate tourney presentations. The Southern California promoter originated the first All Pee-Wee/Junior Karate Championships in 1970, which has gained considerable support from martial artists throughout the West Coast. In 1973, he conceived the Women's Pro/Am Karate Championships, one of the first tournaments in America to award cash prizes to black-belt women contestants in both sparring and form.

Who was the most accomplished female fighter of the 1960s?

Kansas City's Janet Harrison, then Janet Walgren, was the most prominent fighter of her era. Although she competed in karate tournaments before there was such a thing as ratings for women and retired in 1970, Harrison has been cited in every retroactive Top 10 poll published since then. Winning or placing in every tourney she entered, she was the 1966 All American runner-up in

Kansas City's Janet Walgren Harrison (right) was the most prominent female fighter of the 1960s. Here Harrison clashes with Texan Joy Turberville at the '67 U.S. Championships in Dallas.

Oklahoma, a '67 U.S. Championships finalist when disqualified for excessive contact, the 1968 Central States Champion, and the '68 USKA National Champion, and she returned to the U.S. Championships in '68 and won it. In '69, Harrison again won the USKA Grand Nationals and was named the "Women's National Tournament Champion" by the United States Karate Association. The wife of all-time great fighter Jim Harrison, Janet was featured in *Action Karate Magazine* in 1969, a notable honor since women were given little if any publicity at that time. *Official Karate Magazine* also featured her as the premier female competitor of the 1960s.

Who staged the first major karate tournament in Canada?

Toronto's Mas Tsuroka held the Canadian Karate Championships in 1962, which attracted fighters from the United States as well as Canada.

Who won the first major Canadian karate tourney?

New Jersey's Gary Alexander.

Was there a nationally ranked karate fighter who also worked as an undercover narcotics agent?

Yes. Pasadena's Tonny Tulleners was rated eighth in the 1968 *Black Belt Yearbook* Top 10 at about the same time he was serving as an undercover narcotics agent for the Los Angeles Police Department. Tulleners was credited with making several busts and occasionally was forced to use his karate expertise to wade out of dangerous situations. He later moved into other businesses after stating that his undercover work was becoming increasingly more dangerous.

What major incident occurred at the 3rd WUKO World Championships?

Famous French karate champion Dominic Valera physically attacked several officials following his disqualification for excessive contact. He was escorted from the Long Beach Arena by police following the incident. Charges were not pressed against him, but he was denied entry during the remainder of the tournament. Later that same evening, Valera held an impromptu press conference and announced his retirement from noncontact karate in order to compete in professional karate contests exclusively. It's curious to note that while he was viewed as a villain by most of the traditionalists present, he was considered a sort of anti-hero by American karate practitioners.

Who was John Gehlson?

Gehlson, before his tragic death from a heart attack in 1974, was one of the strongest Japanese-style noncontact fighters in the country. A student of Tak

Kubota of Hollywood, Gehlson was a member of the American team at the first WUKO World Karate Championships in Tokyo, Japan.

Who are the members of *Professional Karate's* Hall of Fame?

Since its inception in 1973, *Professional Karate* has named certain individuals to its Hall of Fame by carrying their picture on the back cover, though no actual award has been presented. The nomination was generally accompanied by a feature story or a candid interview with the personality. There are no particular categories. Honorees are chosen for their contributions to the art and/or sport. The winners have been Mike Stone, Joe Lewis, AlGene Caraulia, Bruce Lee, Bill Wallace, Byong Yu, Jhoon Rhee, and Jim Harrison.

What was unique about Byong Yu's career as a karate fighter?

Yu was not only one of the most colorful characters ever to enter the karate ring, but he was also one of the few Orientals to compete successfully in U.S. tournaments. He was twice rated in *Black Belt Magazine's* annual Top 10 poll for fighting, and was ranked among the kata Top 10 in the 1973 *Official Karate Yearbook*. Even more significantly, he achieved all this while in his late thirties.

Why is Fred Wren one of the most frightening opponents to meet in the karate ring?

Known as "The Whirlwind" and "Mean Machine," St. Louis' Fred Wren is one of the meanest fighters in noncontact and semi-contact. A master strategist who knows how to effectively employ scare tactics, the former Texan often psychs out opponents with his aggressive attitude before they even enter the ring. Wren's type of demeanor can quickly intimidate inexperienced foes. Once the match begins, "The Whirlwind" lives up to his name and reputation by pursuing his adversaries with constant forward pressure, all the while unleashing nerve-shattering kiais (yells). His competence, in addition to his tactics, has led him to be rated among *Black Belt Magazine's* Top 10 American fighters for five consecutive years since 1970. In the autumn 1973 issue of *Professional Karate Magazine*, Wren was ranked the number-one semi-contact fighter in the United States. He retired in 1974 because of a knee injury.

What is unique about Glenn Premru's kata record?

Premru is one of two competitors, along with Connecticut's Chuck Merriman, who have successfully competed in black-belt form competition for more than a decade. He won his first title at the Camp LeJeune Karate Championships as a Marine back in 1963. In 1975, based on his performance at the Battle of Atlanta, the sharp technician was rated sixth in the national kata Top 10 by *Professional Karate Magazine*.

What is the most commonly used technique in karate tournaments other than full-contact?

The reverse punch is used more than any other technique, and, consequently, has probably been used to score more points as well.

Who is the only known junior competitor to become a national kata champion in his division?

New York's Eugene Sung. The youngster's form career has spanned the entire United States. His first-place titles include the 1972–75 All American Open at Madison Square Garden, the '73 International Karate Championships in Long Beach, the '74 USKA Grand Nationals in Milwaukee, Wisconsin, the '73 Southwestern Championships in Albuquerque, New Mexico, and the '75 AKA Nationals in Milwaukee. Sung is a student of New York City's William Louie.

Is full-contact sport karate superior to all other types of karate in terms of combat effectiveness?

Not at all. Full-contact karate is conducted under a strict set of rules between skilled professional fighters who wear hand and foot padding. One does not wear pads on the street. Secondly, and most importantly, there exist no combat rules in a street confrontation. Kicks to the groin and knees and open-hand techniques to vital areas, as well as the use of knee and elbow blows, are permissible in self-defense situations. This, of course, is not true in the full-contact karate ring, where rules designed for the participants' safety permit only punches and kicks to specified parts of the body above the belt.

For which techniques is Joe Lewis most noted?

Lewis is particularly noted for his back knuckle and side kick in noncontact karate contests, having renovated the traditional methods of execution. He throws his side kick without much cocking of the knee, and it travels straight from the ground instead of uncocking from a knee held parallel to the ground. Those who insisted there was no power in the kick soon changed their minds when some of Joe's opponents were sent sprawling out of the ring head over heels. Among other innovations in his back knuckle, Lewis used the principle of initial movement. He would execute the technique by moving the hand before the body, thus preventing any telegraphing of the movement. Many times, he threw the back knuckle and returned it so quickly that officials failed to see it and award him the customary point.

Which karate competitor was famous for his front-leg sweep?

France's Dominic Valera was particularly effective with the front-leg sweep in noncontact play. In fact, he used the technique repeatedly throughout his ten-year reign as the European karate king. The heavyweight was so efficient in employing it that his opponents, anticipating the sweep, would often leave themselves open for any other technique, allowing Valera almost to score at will.

Are techniques executed to the groin permissible in sport karate?

Looking at the three levels of sport karate—noncontact, semi-contact and full-contact—groin shots are permitted except in the case of full-contact. Both non-contact and semi-contact rules allow for techniques aimed at the groin with control, and contestants wear protective plastic and sometimes metal cups to guard the area. Because full-contact fighters strike with maximum force, the groin is obviously a restricted area.

Which technique was Chuck Norris most noted for?

Norris was probably best known for his impressive arsenal of kicking techniques. The smooth technician was particularly accurate with a fake front kick turned into a roundhouse kick. The fake generally brought down the opponent's hands, permitting Chuck to hook the roundhouse kick up to his stunned opponent's head.

What distinguishes the Japanese karate competitor from his American counterpart?

Japanese karate players generally practice only one style of karate, while Americans are more likely to study numerous systems. In Japan, where traditional karate reigns, style appears to be given higher consideration than the individual practicing it. American players generally learn all they can from one style, then move into another to enhance their knowledge. This perhaps accounts for the wide range of techniques displayed in U.S. karate tournaments, while Oriental fighters adhere mainly to reverse punches and front kicks.

When was the first karate tournament held in the United States?

The earliest recorded karate tourney in the continental United States was held

One of America's legendary karate fighters, Chuck Norris (right), was best known for his impressive arsenal of kicking techniques. Here he defeats Del Griffith at a tournament in Hawaii.

Tsutomu Ohshima (left), one of the early pioneers of karate in America, demonstrates at one of his first tournaments, held in the late 1950s. At right is Ohshima's student Caylor Adkins, who later became the first AAU Karate Chairman.

in 1958 when Tsutomu Ohshima staged the Neisei Week Karate Championships in Los Angeles. Because of its early date, participation was limited to Ohshima's own students. The event has been promoted annually since its inception and is open only to members of Ohshima's organization, Shotokan Karate of America.

Is Mike Stone noted for any technique?

More than anything else, Stone became famous for his gutsy fighting. Few men at the time possessed his raw courage, and absolutely no one ever felt it was a picnic being in the ring with him. He does, however, attribute his success as a fighter to more intangible elements such as timing and coordination.

Who founded the noncontact type of tournament?

Los Angeles' Tsutomu Ohshima founded noncontact karate in his homeland, Japan, in 1952. That year, when tournament karate competition did not exist anywhere, Ohshima invented an organized system of conducting sport karate matches. As well as formulating the rules structure, he helped originate the policy of using corner judges and a center referee, a practice which he later introduced to the United States in 1958 for his own tournaments. American karate promoters later incorporated and modified Ohshima's methods, but even today, his concepts are still in use in full-contact sport karate.

Who were the karate leaders who originally applied for membership in the Amateur Athletic Union back in the late 1960s?

Arizona's Robert Trias, Washington, D.C.'s Jhoon Rhee, and California's Hidetaka Nishiyama. When karate finally made its bid for official AAU recognition a year or two later, Nishiyama nearly swayed the association in his favor despite much political infighting and cries of prejudice. When the political smoke cleared, however, which took several years, California's Caylor Adkins, a student of karate pioneer Tsutomu Ohshima, was elected the official AAU karate chairman.

What was John Natividad known for during his karate fighting years?

The 1973 Internationals grand champion was cited for his sensational kicking ability. Though people claim he had the fastest feet in the ring other than Bill Wallace's, the retired veteran possessed uncanny deceptiveness more than anything else. Natividad was a master of the lower-body fake. Often, he would initiate an almost imperceptible feint to draw down the opponent's guard and then launch the kick up to the head, making it appear as if he were so fast that the opponent didn't even see the kick in time to attempt to block it.

Who won the first World Karate Championships?

A then unkown brown belt from Hawaii named AlGene Caraulia won the first World Championships, held at the Chicago Coliseum in 1963. It was the first major open karate tournament in the United States. Caraulia later established a karate school in Cleveland, Ohio, where he still operates today.

Who was the grand champion of the first International Karate Championships?

The legendary Mike Stone swept the title in 1964.

Mike Stone (right), one of the three legendary karate fighters of the 1960s, executes a flying side kick against his protégé Steve Fisher.

Bill Wallace (left), a stunning kicker, knocks out Berndt Grothe at the 1971 World Professional Karate Championships. Wallace's title as the world middleweight karate champion was established at the event.

Has anyone ever won the International Karate Championships more than once?

Yes. Mike Stone won the grand title in 1964 and '65; Chuck Norris in '67 and '68; and Joe Lewis in '69, '70 and '71.

What element made the Internationals such an exciting tournament?

The fact that at one time during the 1960s and early 1970s the event attracted all the big-name fighters and form competitors from throughout the United States. Many, many champions were established at the prestigious event. Even the demonstrations were a highlight in themselves. For instance, the late Bruce Lee performed on the Internationals' stage in 1964, a presentation which brought about his discovery by producer William Dozier. The final element was the class of the tournament. Famous celebrities were always in attendance, providing the overall championships with a luster uncommon to most other United States karate events.

Is Bill Wallace's roundhouse kick his best technique?

Yes. The world middleweight champion can use his left foot as Muhammad Ali uses a jab, and Wallace executes the roundhouse kick more than any other technique in his arsenal. His exceptionally fast hook kick runs a close second, however. Wallace knocked out Germany's Bernd Grothe with a hook kick at the World Professional Karate Championships in Los Angeles on his way to gaining the world middleweight crown. In the second defense of his title against Los Angeles' Jem Echollas, Wallace scored a first-round knockdown with his left roundhouse kick.

When did Joe Lewis win his first karate tournament title?

With merely two years of karate experience, Joe burst onto the tournament scene in startling fashion in 1966 by upsetting favored contender Thomas LaPuppet of New York. In the process, Lewis won the grand championship (noncontact) of Jhoon Rhee's National Karate Championships in Washington, D.C. It had been Lewis' first stab at competition and his feat was akin to an amateur golfer winning the U.S. Open in his first pro outing.

Which national karate tournament presented go-go girls among its featured exhibitions of the martial arts?

The 1969 USKA Grand Nationals in Miami, Florida. In between competition and demonstrations the promoters introduced go-go girls and served pizza. According to karate journals reporting the activity, this sole event was responsible for that particular era of karate being dubbed the "sexy sixties."

What is Jeff Smith best known for in the ring?

The fighting style of the world lightheavyweight champion can best be described in one word—rugged—which accounts for his best-known trait. Like Benny Urquidez, Smith is extremely ambidextrous. And yet, like Mike Stone, he is also a gut fighter. A southpaw, Smith has a jarring ridge hand which he employs often with efficient results.

Where was the first karate team event held in the United States?

In 1967, New York's Aaron Banks presented the first team event. One year later, Banks held his second version. He dubbed it the East Coast vs. West Coast Team Championships, and in view of its overwhelming success, other American karate promoters began incorporating the concept into their individual events.

Who were the first team champions in America?

A West Coast team composed of Chuck Norris, Joe Lewis, Steve Sanders, and Jerry Taylor, who were represented by Ed Parker. The losing team, represented by Aaron Banks, was composed of Louis Delgado, Thomas LaPuppet, K. Tanaka, and Joe Hayes.

Did Joe Lewis ever win any kata titles?

Surprisingly (only because of his obvious emphasis on fighting), yes. Lewis won first place in form competition at Jhoon Rhee's 1966 National Karate Championships in Washington, D.C. He performed a kata using the kama, or sickle.

Which technique is Benny Urquidez famous for?

Benny "The Jet" Urquidez, the lightweight world champion of the Professional Karate Association, is not famous for any one particular technique. He has knocked out opponents with a variety of techniques. Urquidez is a spontaneous fighter who hits hard with either hand or foot. His formidable arsenal has gained him a win-loss record of 29–0.

What is the "Eagle Cup"?

The coveted Eagle Cup is the annual award presented by promoter Allen Steen to the winning quintet of the U.S. Karate Team Championships in Dallas, Texas.

What is the Bruce Lee Trophy?

The Bruce Lee Trophy is an annual award given to the outstanding karate player of the year. The prestigious award was conceived by Mike Anderson, publisher of *Professional Karate Magazine,* in 1974. The recipient is determined by the cumulative votes of coaches throughout the United States.

Who have been the recipients of the Bruce Lee Trophy?

Jeff Smith of Washington, D.C., in 1974 and Bill Wallace of Memphis, Tennessee, in 1975.

For what technique was Allen Steen noted?

The king of Texas karate, who reigned as one of the premier fighters of the early 1960s, was perhaps most acclaimed for his slide-up side kick. Steen could unleash devastating power using this technique. He once knocked Kansas City's Jim Harrison 20 feet out of the ring with the kick.

What is the "Gold Cup"?

The Gold Cup is an annual award presented to the most outstanding fighter at Mike Anderson's Top 10 Nationals. When grand championships were still fashionable, where all black-belt divisional winners are pitted together to decide an overall champion, the grand titlist usually won the award. Later on, when this tournament no longer staged a grand championship, the winner of the Gold Cup was determined by the finalist who scored the most points on his way to sweeping his divisional, semi-contact title.

When were grand championships fashionable in karate?

They still are in most amateur karate tournaments in the United States. Since the amount of contact has become a key measure of performance, however, semi-contact and full-contact contests no longer hold such events as a grand championship. The mixing of weight-division finalists to establish one overall champion would probably be disastrous to those in the lower weight categories.

Does Canadian Wally Slocki have a notable technique?

Yes, and a flashy one at that. The unerring Canadian, who was rated the number-one fighter in his homeland for six consecutive years, is known for his unique leg scissors. By leaping in the air and wrapping his legs around the chest of an opponent, Slocki was able to sweep him to the floor. He usually followed up this move with a backward heel stomp from a prone position to gain points in non-contact tournaments.

Who have been the recipients of the "Gold Cup"?

Chicago's Ken Knudson (1971–72), California's Howard Jackson (1973), Oklahoma's Jim Butin (1974), and Ohio's Dave Ruppart (1975).

Who is the only three-time grand champion of the U.S. Karate Championships?

David Moon of Mexico City won the grand title in 1965, '66, and '67.

Is there another three-time winner of the U.S. Karate Championships?

Yes. Memphis' Bill Wallace, who later became the world middleweight champion in full-contact contests, had earlier won the U. S. Championships three times. Wallace victories came in the form of the grand championship titles in 1971 and '73, and in 1974, when promoter Allen Steen no longer held a grand title, Wallace won his middleweight division.

Why full-contact karate?

The sport's most prominent entrepreneur, Mike Anderson, figured it was the only manner in which he could increase spectator interest when he planned his inaugural World Professional Karate Championships in 1974. But even more important, Anderson got wind, he claims, of certain shady characters outside of karate who intended to move in and promote a no-holds-barred, full-contact event, and who also wanted to pit our best fighters against ranked boxers. Anderson says that he urgently felt that if he did not take it upon himself to promote the most dramatic karate event in history and put it on television, the undesirable elements would move in to control the sport.

Who was responsible for getting television coverage for the World Professional Karate Championships in Los Angeles?

Joe Lewis, ironically, the man who earned his heavyweight world title at the same event. Lewis negotiated the original deal with Tom Tannenbaum of Universal Television and brought Mike Anderson in as America's premier karate tournament promoter. More and more, Lewis lost interest and fell out of the picture. By the time the event rolled around in late 1974, Anderson had formed a partnership with Don and Judy Quine of the Professional Karate Association, who finalized the negotiations with Universal.

Did Skipper Mullins use a favorite technique?

The former world professional lightweight karate champ was lauded for his excruciatingly fast roundhouse kick, but he executed the kick differently from Bill Wallace, who depends on relaxed muscles for maximum speed. Possessed of "rubber legs," Mullins could execute vertical side kicks and near-vertical roundhouse kicks. His speed was such that he could often land a roundhouse kick at an opponent's head before the opponent even moved his hands to block it.

Which karate tournament was dedicated to Jim Chapman, a prominent Midwest karate instructor?

The 4th Gateway Open Karate Championships staged in St. Louis, Missouri, in 1971. Promoter Bob Yarnall felt compelled to do so after his friend was killed in a car crash at thirty-three. Black-belt entry fees were converted to a savings bond and presented to six-year-old Jamie Chapman, the late instructor's daughter.

Who was the grand champion of the karate tournament dedicated to the late Jim Chapman?

Glenn Keeney of Anderson, Indiana.

Who were the U.S. fighters selected to represent America in the 2nd WUKO World Karate Championships?

The WUKO (World Union of Karate-Do Organizations) event, held in Paris, France, welcomed the following individuals, even though many Americans claimed that they were not the true representatives of amateur sport karate in the United States: Tonny Tulleners, Frank Smith, James Yabe, John Gehlson, James Field, George Byrd, and Jerry Morrone.

How did "Gentleman Ron" Marchini get his nickname?

The former number-one U.S. fighter from Stockton, California, was deemed "Gentleman Ron" by the martial-arts media because of his sportsmanship.

What are some of the more prominent nicknames given to top regional and national karate competitors?

Howard "The California Flash" Jackson; Benny "The Jet" Urquidez; Dennis "Sugar Bear" Gotcher; Glenn "Mac Truck" McMorris; Ernie "Radar" Smith; Lenny "Whirlwind" Ferguson; Demetrius "The Golden Greek" Havanis; Jeff "The D.C. Bomber" Smith; Bill Wallace ("Fast Billy," "Superfoot," and "The Leg"); Fred Wren ("Whirlwind" and "Mean Machine"); Wally "The Blond Viking" Slocki; John "Giant Killer" Natividad; Everett "Monster Man" Eddy; Glenn "The Fox" Keeney; "Little" John Davis; Ernest "Madman" Russell; Bob "The Voice of Karate" Wall; Roger "The Kansas Warhorse" Carpenter; "Rockin'" Roy Kurban; "Shorty" Mills; Hidy "Mr. Kata" Ochiai; Eric "King of Kata" Lee; Alan "Slick" Miller; Riley "Avenger" Hawkins; Gary "Rabbit" Goodman; Alex "Plus One" Sternberg; "Slippery" Sammy Pace; "Chicken" Gabriel; Melvin "Sugarbear" Hilliard; Phil "The Magnet" Almagno; Ray "Blue Steel" Davis; Donnie "Scorpio" Wright; and "Wildman" Baldwin.

Which technique is Howard Jackson cited for?

Howard Jackson rocketed to stardom as America's number-one semi-contact fighter of 1973, the first black man to do so. His incredibly rapid punching style was as quick as his rise to prominence. Jackson could close the gap between him and his opponent with lightning speed while executing punches in a series until one landed solidly. No matter how big the opponent, Jackson relied on his punching speed to carry him on to an ultimate victory.

What is unique about Steve Sanders' method of fighting in the karate ring?

It is said that the veteran fighter and Black Karate Federation president is the only one who can actualize his kenpo style in noncontact contests. Sanders possesses blinding hand speed, and when he is fighting just about any opponent, observers can quickly identify the inherent kenpo movements. This is remarkable, because fighters generally alter their real fighting style in noncontact; it is not what they would use in actual self-defense. In noncontact, the fastest player can often score the most points. Sanders brilliantly mixes his kenpo training to meet the restrictions of these rules, yet he retains almost to perfection the type of movements one usually identifies more with self-defense encounters than with karate contests.

At which karate tournament did Chuck Norris first rise to fame?

The Winter Nationals in San Jose, California, in November of 1965. Norris defeated Ron Marchini to sweep the grand championship. From this modest start, Norris went on to win every major title in his sport.

Do kung-fu practitioners have their own tournaments in which to compete?

Lately, they are holding their own personal tournaments, which are closed to karate fighters, but it has been frequent for kung-fu competitors to participate in karate tournaments because there are many more of them. Kung-fu advocates often complain that the rules in karate tournaments are unfair to them because of the diverse open-hand techniques often associated with kung-fu movements. There appears to be no solution until kung-fu becomes more popular on a competitive level and establishes tournaments and champions of its own.

What strange incident took place at the 1964 Neisei Week Karate Championships in Los Angeles?

It marked the year that a white belt defeated all comers including black belts to win first-place honors. Promoter Tsutomu Ohshima held only one division, which was open to all belt ranks and weights, instead of categorizing the tournament. Hayward Nishioka, a white-belt beginner in karate, but a national black-belt judo champion, intelligently used his judo expertise within the constraints of the rules. He used a judo leg sweep followed by a karate reverse punch to outpoint all his noncontact opponents and stun everyone in attendance with his performance.

Who is Carlos Bunda?

Bunda took the lightweight title of the first International Karate Championships back in 1964. But since his victory in the early blood-and-guts era of American sport karate, he has remained relatively behind the scenes.

For which technique was Ken Knudson noted?

The Chicago karate king was abhorred in the ring because of his unorthodox shin-to-shin sweep. Instead of sweeping the back of the opponent's leg with his leg as is more conventional, Knudson would ram his shin into his opponent's shin. The technique was successful for the former Top 10-ranked national fighter, and painful for those victimized by it.

Will karate ever be included as part of the Olympic Games?

The first step in winning Olympic recognition was taken in 1975 when application was made to the General Assembly of International Federations (GAIF), the governing body of all sports. Because karate advocates couldn't get together and decide among themselves which group should be the official organization to apply, karate will not be included at the World Games in 1977. Both the World Union of Karate-Do Organizations (WUKO) and the International Amateur Karate Federation, a secondary organization not officially recognized by the general karate community, applied for official recognition. GAIF rejected both groups as well as applications from the World Tae Kwon Do Federation and the International Tae Kwon Do Federation. Too many groups, as Caylor Adkins, chairman of the AAU karate committee, points out.

Adkins said that if one group had applied, the GAIF might have accepted karate, which would have meant entry into the World Games in 1977. In 1976, however, both karate and tae kwon do were accepted for entry into GAIF, which could lead to possible acceptance in the 1984 Olympics.

Who is the valid representative of amateur karate in the United States?

Though other groups are making claims as the official organ, the Amateur Athletic Union (AAU) became the official representative in 1973.

Why were colored uniforms developed for karate competitors?

Before this innovation, karate competitors wore either a black or a white gi, or combinations of both. Karate entrepreneur Mike Anderson adopted colored gis in 1974 as part of his historic World Professional Karate Championships in Los Angeles. According to Anderson, he merely stole the concept from other major sports in order to put more excitement in karate competition for observers. He now sells an entire line of colored uniforms through his company, Universal Imports of America, in Oklahoma City.

What is the standard ring size for karate competition?

In most cases the size of the ring is determined by the size of the facility in which the event is taking place. Usually, 20 feet square is used as a guideline.

What is Jhoon Rhee's Safe-T Equipment made of?

The hand and foot pads which helped revolutionize professional sport karate are made of foam rubber.

Safe-T Equipment, as worn on the hands and feet of the above contestants, was developed for protection against possible injury in sport karate.

Why was Safe-T Equipment invented?

Safe-T Equipment, invented by karate pioneer Jhoon Rhee of Washington, D.C., was developed for the sole purpose of adding more excitement to professional sport karate competition by safely permitting the use of moderate to full contact. Before its development in 1973, the rules used in sport karate stipulated only noncontact, where all blows to the face were pulled and only light body contact was permissible. Rhee's introduction of foam-rubber protective gear revolutionized the sport and, once established at Mike Anderson's Top 10 National Karate Championships that year, initiated semi-contact professional karate. Anderson later staged in Los Angeles his World Professional Karate Championships, where he used Rhee's Safe-T Equipment to establish full-contact sport karate.

What critical event jeopardized sport karate in the United States?

On July 11, 1975, Act 1-31, the District of Columbia Boxing and Wrestling Commission Act, was made law by the Council of the District of Columbia. This law established a District of Columbia Boxing and Wrestling Commission to govern boxing, wrestling, and the martial arts in that state. The commission had the authority to promulgate rules and regulations to regulate boxing, wrestling, and the martial arts within its jurisdiction. Martial arts was defined as karate, judo, kung-fu, jujutsu, tae kwon do, aikido, and other such forms of self-defense, sport, or weaponry. The commission, to be composed of three who were not martial artists, was vested with the sole direction, management, control, and jurisdiction over all boxing, wrestling, and martial-arts contests, matches, exhibitions, and showings, professional as well as amateur, to be conducted, held, given, or shown within the District of Columbia.

The act further specified that it would collect and set fees for annual licenses to participants, and would also collect 5 percent of all gate receipts and 10 percent from closed-circuit or subscription television. The law was in the act of being spread to the state of Maryland when a strange thing happened. The letter to the Maryland Boxing Commissioner was sent by mistake to tae kwon do pioneer Jhoon Rhee of Washington, D.C. Using the influence of his political contacts in high government offices, Rhee was able to reverse the controversial law.

The act would have set a precedent for the entire nation, because the District of Columbia is the only region where bills have to pass through both the U.S. Senate and the House of Representatives. The controversial act jeopardized the martial arts because it would have taken control out of the hands of the very people who make their livelihoods from them. D.C. martial artists were not even aware of the passing of the law, even though it would have directly affected their businesses.

Shortly after the incident, a similar law was passed in California, placing professional sport karate under the jurisdiction of the State Athletic Commission, which also governs professional boxing and wrestling. The commission took command when several professional-karate fiascos were broadcast on national television.

What is professional kata?

Professional kata is the most recent innovation in sport karate. Competitors, primarily black belts, vie for cash prizes using more flamboyant techniques. The pro kata format, established by Mike Anderson at his 1974 Top 10 Nationals in St. Louis, provided a new dimension for form contestants who had competed the same way for the past ten years. By awarding prize money and holding a triple elimination before deciding four finalists, the excitement and drama of the event were strongly enhanced. In 1975, prominent karate sportswriter John Corcoran was instrumental in permanently establishing the concept by influencing major tournament directors across the U.S. to adopt professional kata as part of their regular events. The event could rightly be compared to the freestyle division in professional skating, in which performers aren't restricted to prearranged routines.

Who were and are some of the top form competitors in U.S. karate competition?

The 1973 Official Karate Yearbook featured the first ratings for kata competitors. The listing, done alphabetically, included Al Dacascos (California), George Dillman (Pennsylvania), Eric Lee (California), Chuck Merriman (Connecticut), Toyataro Miyazake (New York), Glenn Premru (Florida), Jim Roberts, Jr. (Maryland), Alex Sternberg (New York), Mike Stone (Nevada), and Byong Yu (California). Honorable mention was given to Steve Fisher (California), Bob Bowles (Indiana), Louis Delgado (New York), and William Louie (New York).

Since the introduction of *Professional Karate Magazine's* Top 10 kata ratings in December 1974, the following competitors have been ranked: Hidy Ochiai (New York), Alex Kwok (Canada), Lawrence Kuss (Maryland), Ron Shaw (Ohio), Tayari Casel (New Jersey), Walt Bone (Florida), Glenn Premru, Malia Dacascos (California), Bob Bowles, Hiro Hamada (Virginia), Bill Odom (Maryland), Jim Roberts, Jr. (Maryland), Jerry Li (Florida), Randy Holman (Illinois), Roger Tung (Washington), Minobu Miki (California), Chong Lee (California), Al Leong (California), James Cook (Ohio), Alex Sternberg, and Steve Fisher.

What was the Capitol Hill Grudge Bout?

Along with Jhoon Rhee's Washington vs. Dominican Republic team karate matches in 1975, he presented a special politician's semi-contact division pitting a trio of Democrats against a Republican threesome. Presented under the auspices of Rhee's World Blackbelt League, the novel division featured Democrats Rep. Walter Fauntroy (D.C.), Rep. Tom Bevill (Alabama), and Sen. Quentin Burdick (North Dakota) against Republicans Rep. Willis Grandison, Jr. (Ohio), Rep. Floyd Spence (South Carolina), and Sen. Ted Stevens (Alaska).

The members of the U.S. Congress appeared on behalf of the Freedom of the Press Foundation. But they didn't just make an appearance. The politicians kicked and punched each other in delighted glee. When the smoke cleared, the teams fought to a hearty standoff. The participants are members of Rhee's twice-weekly classes and have come to be known as the "Capitol Hill karate corps." Pulitzer

Prize–winning journalist Jack Anderson made this comment in a *Parade* cover story prior to the event: "The 94th Congress, it may be said, has not produced much legislation, but it is generating a lot of excitement. As Senator Burdick told us, 'Karate is one of the best things we do on the Hill.'"

Which famous karate champion appeared on TV's *Superstars?*

World middleweight champion Bill Wallace appeared in the third set of eliminations on January 31, 1976, which was broadcast one week later nationwide on ABC TV. Wallace finished tenth among eleven of America's most respected athletes, including Gary Swann of the Pittsburgh Steelers and world-rated heavyweight boxer Ken Norton. It was the first real endorsement the sport received from major outside sources.

Which karate contest was termed the "great rematch"?

The second fight between Canada's Wally Slocki and world lightheavyweight champ Jeff Smith of Washington, D.C. Smith had defeated Slocki to win his title in September 1974 at the World Professional Karate Championships in Los Angeles. Some observers, however, considered it a controversial decision. Battle of Atlanta promoter Joe Corley scheduled the "great rematch" on February 8, 1976. Smith once again proved his superiority by winning a nine-round decision over the tough Canadian. The match later appeared on the national sports show *Champions* on April 10.

What is the Professional Karate Association?

Conceived in late August 1974, the PKA held its World Professional Karate Championships to launch full-contact competition. The object of the organization was to establish karate as a major professional sport with recognizable champions, standardized rules, and television network coverage for its events. The original principals were Mike Anderson and Don and Judy Quine. Anderson evacuated his post as executive vice-president in June 1975 to form a similar association, the World Martial Arts Council. The PKA has held five major events since its WPKC in 1974.

What is the World Blackbelt League?

Formed on May 1, 1975, by an eminent group of sports enthusiasts, the World Blackbelt League is a professional martial-arts team concept, and intends to conduct full-contact competition on a regular basis among eight teams in major cities throughout the Western Hemisphere. Founded by Jhoon Rhee and head-quartered in Washington, D.C., the WBL includes martial ballet (team kata) competition as well as full-contact fighting.

What is the prime age for a karate competitor?

The prime age range is eighteen to twenty-nine, although it depends on the individual athlete and the type of karate contest he indulges in. Maryland's Mike Warren was already successful in noncontact karate at age sixteen. Indiana's Parker Shelton, at thirty-five, was still winning titles in semi-contact karate. World heavyweight champ Joe Lewis of California engaged in full-contact matches at thirty-two.

Who is Tom Carroll?

Better known as Thomas LaPuppet, Carroll was one of the most consistent fighters of the 1960s. He changed his surname after being nicknamed "The Puppet."

How did Thomas LaPuppet get his name?

As a green belt, he would perform a puppet routine while sparring as if he were being manipulated by the pull of unseen strings. His performance became so popular that, as a joke, he registered at his first karate tournament as Tom LaPuppet. Tom won the brown-belt championship and subsequently gained media recognition as Tom LaPuppet. The name has stuck with him ever since.

What is the "Friendship Trophy"?

The Friendship Trophy was presented to Ed Parker, tournament director of the International Karate Championships, by Dr. Olaf Simon of Calgary, Alberta, Canada, in 1968 as a symbol of international friendship in karate. Also known as the "perpetual cup," the trophy is awarded to each grand champion of the Internationals to keep for a period of one year, or until he relinquishes the title. Originally, those champions who repeat as grand champion two years in succession were accorded the additional honor of having their names permanently engraved on the trophy. But since sport karate has grown so drastically since then, every grand champ, regardless of how many times he repeats his performance, has his name inscribed on the Friendship Trophy.

Which names have been inscribed on the Friendship Trophy?

Mike Stone (1964 and '65), Allen Steen ('66) Chuck Norris ('67 and '68), Joe Lewis (1969, '70, and '71), Darnell Garcia ('72), John Natividad ('73), Jeff Smith ('74), Lenny Ferguson ('75), and Ray Sua ('76).

Can women compete against men in karate competition?

In a report in the April 1976 issue of *Karate Illustrated,* it was pointed out that women cannot compete against men in an all-out streetfight because, pound for pound, women do not possess the raw power of men. In actual sport competition, however, women have been known on occasion to defeat men, especially in form competition, or in noncontact, point-type tournaments. However, some negligent promoters have pitted man against woman in full-contact karate. In most cases, the women sustained numerous injuries and/or were knocked out.

Where is kick-boxing most popular?

In Thailand, its native country, where it is a national pasttime and sport.

What has been the highest purse awarded to a full-contact karate fighter?

The largest purse to date has been $5,000. This amount has only been awarded to some of the established world champions. Those who have won $5,000 for a single fight are Bill Wallace, Jeff Smith, and Benny Urquidez.

Why are there so many karate tournaments in the United States?

Because there has been no central organization which supervises who can throw a tournament where and when. The karate industry, then, having no real quality control, does not self-regulate the promotion of tournaments. Furthermore, since karate promoters are principally studio owners who diversify to make an adequate living, most of the karate tournaments staged, except full-contact, are individual, one-time ventures.

What was unusual about the 1974 Beverly Hills Pro/Am Karate Championships?

The tournament attracted among its spectators more Hollywood celebrities than any other event in the history of karate. Among those attending were Herb

Alpert, James Caan, Jack Nicholson, producer David Wolper, movie theater mogul Ted Mann, Jim Kelly, Raymond St. Jacques, Irene Tsu, Lalo Schifrin, and Aldo Ray. The event was promoted by Creative Action, a company operated by Stuart Sobel and Emil Farkas.

Who was the sole female in 1975 to place in karate's triple crown?

Maryanne Corcoran. She started the first leg of her national debut by winning third place in form at the Battle of Atlanta, and she capped off the year with second-place finishes at the prestigious International Karate Championships in Long Beach, California, and the Top 10 Nationals in Anderson, Indiana. Her record was not duplicated by any other female champion that year.

◀ Hollywood's Maryanne Corcoran, rated among the top four female kata competitors of 1975, is also the wife of black belt John Corcoran. They are among the few husband-and-wife black belts in the United States.

Kung-fu

Thanks to the late Bruce Lee, kung-fu's influence was felt on a worldwide level. Even though the deceased superstar didn't really practice kung-fu per se, his short but colorful film career arrived simultaneously with the explosion of the so-called "Eastern Westerns." In combination with the Kung Fu TV series, kung-fu found its way into the heart of America through the television and motion-picture industries. Needless to say, the resulting confusion made it virtually impossible to interpret exactly what kung-fu was all about.

Because of its inherent diversity and the scarcity of written matter, the authors have attempted to sift fact from rumor regarding this ancient art. Unlike karate, or, for that matter, any other martial art, kung-fu still appears to be highly mysterious, even in modern times. In fact, its true nature has been explored only recently. Here, for the first time, is some of the up-to-date information on this little-known science, which every martial artist should find valuable and fascinating.

What do animals have to do with kung-fu?

The movements of animals have been the basis of many martial arts, most notably kung-fu. It is believed that ancient kung-fu masters studied not only the movements of animals, but more specifically, their reactions during battle with other animals. The masters then adapted and developed these movements to fit

Sifu Doug Wong demonstrating one of the many animal forms associated with the practice of kung-fu.

man's own method of combat. Psychological principles were also learned in these studies. For example, it was noted that an animal as small as a cat could easily defeat a larger animal because of the cat's instinctive thrust of a claw to the eyes. This the masters developed as an open-hand slash to the eyes using the points of the fingers.

The movements of the bird, bear, monkey, tiger, and deer, specifically, formed the basis of Hua To's exercises, which he devised in the second century A.D. The noted surgeon developed these exercises to relieve emotional stress and to tone the body. They were later altered for combative purposes.

How does Chinese boxing differ from Western boxing?

Chinese boxing, also known as kung-fu, encompasses the use of the entire body and holds few restrictions on exactly which techniques can be used in combat. Western boxing, since it is promoted as a sport or an occupation, limits the fighter to the use of his hands, which are protected by padded gloves.

What is the difference between kung-fu and gung-fu?

The *g* in gung-fu and the *k* in kung-fu result from dialectic variations of the Chinese language. A Cantonese pronounces the word as gung-fu, and a Mandarin pronounces it as kung-fu. The spelling of the word is altered only when it is written or pronounced in the Cantonese or Mandarin tongue. However, both have the same meaning.

Does the word "kung-fu" have a flowery meaning like so many other Oriental fighting disciplines?

Surprisingly, it doesn't. Literally translated, "kung-fu" has a variety of meanings—"time"; "strength"; "ability"; "skill"; "work"; and "task"—none of these obviously considered flowery. "Kung-fu" is defined as a period used by a person to perform a specific type of task, ability, or work. In the Western Hemisphere, "kung-fu" is a generic term used to refer to the Chinese martial arts exclusively.

How important are the "inner" teachings of kung-fu as opposed to its "outer" teachings?

According to just about every instructor of the craft, the inner teachings are much more important than the physical techniques. While almost anyone can perfect the outer form of kung-fu, the hand and foot movements, few can master its inner understanding. *Karate Illustrated Magazine* once reported on a 107-year-old kung-fu grand master who, though he barely had the strength to stand, still possessed uncanny inner power. According to the story, this grand master could use his inner power to make a man standing across the room stagger back and forth, just by lifting his hand. Whether this story is true or not, it does point out how those who practice kung-fu for lengthy periods feel about the inner understanding one must have of the art.

How many different kinds of kung-fu are there?

There are hundreds of subdivisions in kung-fu. The exact number is not known. These subdivisions, or styles, include those taught in China, Japan, Korea, and the United States. Much like the styles of karate or other martial arts, each system of kung-fu differs from its counterparts in its origin, its founder, and which movements are essential to it.

Can one be too old to learn kung-fu?

No. The television series *Kung Fu* has been responsible for the belief that one must start to learn kung-fu at a very young age. However, one can extract benefits from kung-fu, whether they be physical techniques or philosophy, at any age.

Is kung-fu a religion?

Absolutely not. Many tend to confuse kung-fu with Buddhism, which grew along with kung-fu in the Buddhist monasteries of China. Part of this belief comes from the television series, which linked the two together. Kung-fu can better be described as a way of life. Once learned, many of its inherent philosophies can be utilized in everyday life. In that light, some extremely serious practitioners do consider it their personal religion.

Is kung-fu still practiced in China now that it is a Communist country?

Kung-fu is known and practiced in China as wu shu, and it is considered more a physical exercise than anything else. The inner teachings have been momentarily overlooked in favor of physical disciplines, and surprisingly so in a country where myth and mystery abound. It is especially avoided as a military fighting art, according to a spokesman for the wu shu troupe which toured the United States in 1974.

Does one have to speak Chinese to learn kung-fu?

The terminology used in most commercial American kung-fu kwoon (training halls) is the English counterpart of the Chinese terms. However, much of the terminology is Chinese when one begins to advance in the learning stages. Some instructors in the Chinatowns throughout the United States speak only Chinese. However, what is really necessary is being able to communicate with the instructor, and this can often be accomplished to some degree by his physical examples.

Would it be better to learn kung-fu in the Orient?

It might be, depending on the ability of the instructor and whether or not he is willing to teach you. Few Caucasians are openly accepted as students in the Orient. Even in the United States, it took many years before the Oriental kung-fu masters would open their doors to members of other races. Additionally, one may find the discipline and pace a little too rugged in the Orient, for the teachers are much stricter. It is much more convenient to learn kung-fu close to one's home, at least in the United States, because there instructors are much more acclimated to the more casual lifestyle of Americans.

How many kung-fu experts are there in America?

The exact number is not known, but there are probably several hundred at the time of this writing. Most of them teach in the Chinatown sections, such as in Los Angeles, San Francisco, and New York. Due to the great number of Chinese now residing in the United States, many of whom are probably very efficient at kung-fu but do not teach it, it is extremely difficult to estimate the number of experts. A problem developed on the heels of the kung-fu boom during the early and middle 1970s when phony operators professed to be proficient at the art.

Does one have to dedicate himself completely to kung-fu to learn it?

One would have to surrender all creature comforts and totally devote himself to kung-fu only if he planned to enter a monastery. A student does have to dedicate himself by taking his study seriously and working hard to achieve skill, but he doesn't have to practice all day every day. For the average working man or woman, one or two hours per day three times a week is average. In addition, a short workout at least once every day will further skill, but will never make one a master. It is generally said that to attain the level of kung-fu proficiency for effective fighting or self-defense, at least seven years of almost daily devotion and arduous training are required. This, of course, would vary according to individual ability.

What is the "iron palm"?

The iron palm is a method reputedly enabling one to produce a psychophysical heat internally, and with voluntary control, made to project into the palms of the hands or to other areas of the body. The palm is a primary striking point of the hand and is a part of the body to which many Chinese mythical legends are connected, one of which is the iron palm. The training necessary to manifest the iron palm, however, is so rigorous that there is doubt as to whether or not modern practitioners have been able to achieve the real thing. In ancient times, this method is reputed to have bordered on the ability to possess the "death touch" in combat. In contemporary martial arts, any practitioner who achieves a hand like iron, so to speak, is credited with possessing an iron palm. So far, there is no concrete proof that the death touch really exists.

Kung-fu, unlike many of the other martial arts, is still practiced primarily by the Chinese, who maintain the traditional methods of physical and spiritual development.

Kung-fu has both internal and external applications. Here Eric Lee (right) demonstrates the use of an external technique on his opponent.

What is the difference between the internal and external systems of Chinese boxing?

An external Chinese boxing system is basically defined as any system which emphasizes the training of bones and muscles. As its name implies it has to do with external forces and principles of motion. Advocates of an external system usually adhere to linear techniques.

An internal Chinese boxing system is any which emphasizes the regulation of breath, and which unifies hard and soft techniques, although internal advocates also maintain the training of bones and muscles. Users of the latter system generate power from internal sources, which they are then able to apply externally. Devotees of the internal systems of kung-fu generally adhere to a defensive, circular approach to fighting.

Who was the first man on the West Coast to teach kung-fu openly to non-Orientals?

In 1964, Ark Y. Wong broke the traditional kung-fu "color line" by opening up his Wah Que Studio in Los Angeles' Chinatown to anyone who was interested in learning his art. Previously, the art was reserved exclusively for full-blooded Chinese. Currently, members of any race can learn kung-fu except at a few secluded studios in the old Chinatowns across America where it is still felt that only Chinese should learn the ancient martial art.

What are some of the better-known Chinese kung-fu systems?

Some of the more prevalent arts are tai-chi chuan, Shaolin, pa-kua, various forms of kenpo, choy li-fut, hsing-i, hung-gar, nie-chia, white crane, and wing-chun.

What is choy li-fut?

A southern Chinese style of kung-fu. It stems from the Sil Lum Temple (better known as the Shaolin Temple) of fifth-century China. Choy li-fut is essentially a long-range style of boxing relying heavily on strong horse stances.

Who is the founder of the wing-chun style of kung-fu?

According to historians, wing-chun was founded by Yim Wing Chun, a female who created the martial art after studying under a Buddhist nun some four hundred years ago. It is the only known martial art to have been founded by a woman. Literally translated, "wing-chun" means "beautiful springtime."

What is the colorful legend accompanying graduation from the Shaolin temple, the birthplace of the Chinese martial arts?

The legend concerns the obstacles undertaken by a student wishing to graduate from the famous monastery. According to legend, he must pass three tests. The first was supposedly a complex oral examination covering the history, theory, and significant thought of kung-fu. Then the student had to work his way through an intricate boobytrapped hallway. As the story goes, 108 wooden dummies armed with spears, clubs, and knives attacked him as he triggered mechanical devices under the floor with his own weight. Next, he was forced to lift with his forearms a 500-pound smoldering urn, which burnt into his flesh two indelibly sculptured symbols of a tiger and a dragon. Only then was the student free, a graduate branded with the trademark of his alma mater.

What is the formal title of a kung-fu teacher?

His title is sifu (pronounced *see*-foo), meaning "teacher" or "instructor." A female instructor is called simu (*see*-moo).

How did the study of herbal medicine become synonymous with kung-fu?

Since sparring and actual combat brought about a wide range of injuries, it became mandatory for early kung-fu practitioners to learn traditional Chinese medicine. Initially, these advocates concentrated principally on ointments and baths which toughened the skin and body. Additionally, they learned basic skills such as bonesetting and caring for open wounds. Later, many practitioners realized that a fighter was only as strong as his health, so emphasis was placed on a more suitable approach to medicine. Greater significance was accorded preventive medicine, particularly exercise systems designed to keep the internal functions of the body smoothly working.

Acupuncture and pressure points, originally taught as body target areas because of their crippling capacity, were studied for the purpose of maintaining bodily strength and treating disease. Thus, herbal preparations came into use to strengthen external weaknesses. In contemporary kung-fu, most masters retain the practice of herbal medicines and pass this knowledge on to their students as a required part of the curriculum.

What is acupuncture and how is it related to the martial arts?

Acupuncture is a traditional Chinese therapeutic technique. Needles are placed in certain key points of the body in order to cure specific illnesses or injuries. It is usually included as part of the healing arts studied by kung-fu practitioners.

Why was kung-fu not originally taught to people outside the Chinese race?

According to passages from Alex Ben Block's *The Legend of Bruce Lee,* "The reason stems back to the Boxer Rebellion in China just after the turn of the century. After increasing foreign exploitation from 1870 on, many Chinese began forming secret martial arts societies to rid themselves of the 'foreign devils.' By about 1900 the art of kung-fu had reached a sophisticated level of perfection and an acceptance approaching religious frenzy.

"The forty-year foreign rape of China followed (following the Boxer Rebellion), until Mao Tse-tung took over in 1949. After the rebellion a general rule that kung-fu should be taught only to thoroughbred Chinese became an unwritten, sworn law."

What is Chinese kenpo?

Introduced in 1954 by Ed Parker, kenpo, or Chinese kenpo as it is more appropriately known, is widely assumed to have been the first style of the Chinese arts taught publicly in the continental United States. Yet, as a derivative of kosho-ryu (*koh*-show-ryoo), meaning "old pine tree style," it wasn't considered kung-fu at all, even though many of its moves are linear. At least, not in the Okinawan sense. The traditional art of the Mitose family of Japan, kosho-ryu kenpo traces its roots to the even older Shaolin kung-fu, kenpo being the Japanese pronunciation of the Chinese characters for *chuan fa* (pronounced *chwawn*-fa), meaning fist or boxing. Bringing Shaolin kung-fu to Japan before the sixteenth century, the Mitose family members cultivated all aspects of the art until it developed into the distinctive kosho-ryu. Parker's brand of kenpo is now one of the leading systems having a Chinese influence practiced in the United States.

Who are known as the "dynamic duo" of kung-fu?

Californians Al Leong and James Lew, two students of prominent West Coast sifu Douglas Wong. The pair received rave notices from the martial-arts media for their flamboyant weapons demonstrations at the '73 and '74 International Karate Championships in Long Beach, California. Based on these performances, the title of "dynamic duo" caught on quickly.

How exactly did kung-fu influence different systems of karate?

The northern styles of kung-fu influenced the Koreans in the development of kicking techniques. The southern styles, stressing hand techniques, laid the basis for modern karate, which was later developed in Okinawa.

How was the praying-mantis system of kung-fu developed?

The system had its beginning at the famed Shaolin Temple in the northern Chinese province of Honan. As the story goes, one day the master Wong Long accidentally came upon a praying mantis in the heat of instinctive battle with a cicada, and from there developed the principle that accompanies the fighting of the praying-mantis system. The style lacked footwork, however, so Wong Long copied the footwork of the monkey. In the final analysis he combined seventeen other arts and grouped them into the praying-mantis system, which became the most advanced style taught at the Shaolin Temple.

How was the praying-mantis system divided?

As the years passed the system was broken down into the northern praying mantis, geared to facilitate fighting on the open plains of northern China, and the southern praying mantis, more suitable for confrontations on the congested streets and narrow alleyways of southern China.

What is one of the easier kung-fu styles to learn?

Wing-chun. Its overall simplicity is reflected in the total number of forms one is required to learn in the style—three! In one way or another, all wing-chun techniques are contained within the sil lim tao ("little idea"), the chum kil ("searching for the bridge"), and the bil jee ("shooting fingers"). Because of this simplicity, wing-chun is considered one of the easiest kung-fu systems to learn. It sometimes takes about one year to gain a reasonable measure of proficiency, but mastery of the simplicity invariably takes years.

How is the "sticky hands" exercise of wing-chun kung-fu performed?

Sticky hands, or more technically, chi sao (chee-*sow*), is used to develop sensitivity in the hands and arms of the practitioner. With the hands and wrists lightly touching the opponent's, the practitioners balance each other's forward motions with a rocking motion. Neither practitioner can move his hands forward without telegraphing his intentions. Thus, a student learns to detect the intentions of his opponent by feel. Some proficient chi sao experts can perform the exercise while blindfolded, and without any sort of prearrangement, they can repeatedly check their opponent's moves while simultaneously striking him at will.

Are there any accredited kung-fu classes in college?

Only one that is widely known. George Long of San Francisco teaches white crane kung-fu at the University of California at Berkeley as a five-unit philosophy course.

There has been much written and spoken about the five animals whose movements were imitated to form the basis of kung-fu. How is each animal imitated?

The crane, based on exercises to strengthen the sinews, stresses balance and quick foot movements; while the dragon, from exercises for the spirit, emphasizes flexibility and graceful movement. On the other hand, the leopard, a development of exercises to increase strength, is based on power and is different from the tiger, a clawing-type style built upon exercises for the bones. Finally, the snake, based on exercises for development of chi (*chee*), or inner power, is a method of pinpoint striking of vital body targets.

Why is the horse stance so heavily emphasized in kung-fu training?

The horse stance, in which a practitioner extends his legs laterally with the knees bent as if straddling a horse, is considered the most important part of kung-fu training. It is believed that one must first learn how to stand before learning to walk, then run, then jump. Before any kung-fu technique can be executed properly, one must be able to use the horse stance in union with the hands, for without leg action, the upper part of the body has no power, kung-fu instructors contend. Some stricter traditional kung-fu styles are only taught after the student practices the painful horse stance for a period of as much as one year. This could mean daily training in which a student assumes the horse stance for perhaps several hours. Most American kwoon (training halls) have a more lenient regulation, however.

Judo

Judo, although not the oldest of the martial arts, was the first to reach outside the Orient to the Western world, where it became at first a fascinating, secretive fighting art and later an internationally recognized sport. By the beginning of World War II, there were judo schools in almost every major country, and following the war, it became a recognized Olympic sport.

Founded by Professor Jigoro Kano in the late 1800s, judo is by far the most organized and structured of the many martial arts. But, having its origin in the Orient, much of its mystery and secrecy still needs to be brought to light. In this chapter, some of these mysteries will be explored and explained for all to understand. The courtesies, customs, and philosophy play as much a part in judo as the actual physical combat.

How many black-belt ranks are there in judo?

While most martial arts have ten black-belt ranks, judo has twelve.

What is a breakfall?

A breakfall is a method of safely falling to the ground upon being thrown by an opponent or partner. There are several variations, including front and rear

◀ Because of the harsh falls a judo student must take, his most important phase of learning lies in the proper methods of applying breakfalls.

breakfalls. In each case, the hands and arms are flung outward and downward to disperse the shock of the fall.

What is the Kodokan?

The Kodokan (*koh*-da-kawn) was the world's first judo school, founded by Jigoro Kano in Tokyo in 1882. Upon its opening it had merely nine students. Today, its members number in the millions, and the Kodokan is considered the mecca for all judo practitioners.

Who founded judo?

Judo, or "gentle way," is a method of unarmed combat developed from jujutsu by Jigoro Kano. Kano established his judo in such a way that it embraces five stages of instruction, each containing eight throws. For every throw there exists a proper counterthrow involving definite principles of motion.

Why is the judo uniform made as it is?

For practicality. The judogi (*jew*-doe-ghee), as it is called, is easy to keep clean and is white because, traditionally, this represents purity. The judogi is as close as one can get to street clothing without dangerous objects or materials such as buttons, belts, leather, and zippers. It is made of strong, heavyweight material to permit the free use of powerful techniques and to endure the constant pulling motions of an opponent or partner. It is loose-fitting, as are most karate and kung-fu uniforms, to accommodate free movement, and the sleeves and legs are short so as not to hinder hand and foot movements.

Is it true that judo techniques would not work against an opponent who did not have on heavy clothing to grasp?

No. Most judo techniques can be applied by grasping the adversary's body instead of his clothes. Judo instructors often prove this by having students work without the judogi top. In place of the sleeve, the usual grasping point, the opponent's wrist is held, then the thrower's arm is passed under his opponent's upper arm or around his body instead of grasping the lapel to throw him.

Is judo a religion?

No. Judo does not teach a set of beliefs about the origin and structure of the universe, or about God and his relations with man. It therefore cannot be called a religion in the common meaning of the word. However, judo, like other martial arts, is a way of approaching life. Moral training is inherent. Dogmatic rigidity is not.

If a judo practitioner defeats a higher-ranked judoka in a contest, does he automatically take over his rank?

No. Victories won against others in a tournament contest do have something to do with rank advancement in some cases, but a judoka who may suffer a defeat in a contest cannot have his rank taken away.

Can Kodokan rank, once given, be taken away?

Yes, but only in cases of disgrace to Kodokan judo. If a practitioner turns professional and either makes false displays or engages in contests as a prizefighter, he can be expelled from judo altogether. In addition, then, his rank and registration will be deleted. One former All-Japan champion has been expelled from Kodokan judo for this reason. However, a man who, for various reasons, is unable to maintain his skill, stamina, and strength, and who can be beaten by a younger contestant, is assumed to have been worth his rank when he won it. He can be honored for his past performance as a competitor much like other retired, former championship-level athletes. Besides, most high-ranking retired judoka continue to teach their craft. Thus, they still contribute to the growth of the art and sport.

Can high-ranking judoka still defeat tournament champions in spite of their advanced age?

No. The strongest tournament competitors are the ones who win championships. Many fine contestants continue to enter tournaments until they reach their mid-thirties, but for the most part, the champions are in their twenties. As the champions age they are aware that they have passed their athletic peak. They then usually retire to teach or otherwise contribute to judo. However, many of these retired 6th-, 7th-, and 8th-degree black belts are in their fifties and sixties and can still defeat younger, lower-ranked practitioners because of their experience and knowledge.

What is the meaning of the red-and-white lapel pin worn by judoka?

It is the official insignia of Kodokan judo. An old Japanese legend relates the use of a giant eight-sided mirror to bring back the light to a darkened earth. Thus, the Kodokan pin is the symbol of deliverance and achievement. The mirror is called yata no kagami (*yaw*-ta know ka-*gaw*-mee), or "eight-headed dragon mirror." It is white, which signifies purity and clearness of thinking, without jealousy or hatred, forgetful of evil. Within the mirror is the heart of burning red, symbolizing the judoka's burning zeal and determination to master techniques and perfect his character.

Why are Japanese terms used in judo?

Japanese is the international language of judo. One doesn't refer to the fencing foil as a sword. One doesn't use the term "crooked race" in skiing, but rather, "slalom." Many sports which find their origin in foreign countries use non-English terms. Without using Japanese terminology in judo for reference and instruction, judoka of different nations could hardly communicate, it is largely believed.

What is the ultimate goal of judo?

As defined by founder Jigoro Kano, the harmonious development and eventual perfection of human character.

What are the three factors composing a judo throw?

Kuzushi (ku-*zoo*-she) meaning "off balance," tsukuri (tsue-*core*-ee), or "entry," and atemi waza (aw-*tem*-ee *waw*-za), or "execution."

What is the yudanshakai?

The yudanshakai (you-*dawn*-sha-kye) is an association of black belts chartered by the Kodokan, which administers judo. The name means "black-belt holders' group" and can refer to any organization of black belts in the martial arts, but it is usually more closely associated with judo.

Has anyone ever reached the coveted 12-degree black belt in judo?

No. Not even Jigoro Kano, the founder of judo, held the 12th-degree black belt.

How big is the Kodokan, and where is it located?

It is a seven-story building located in the Suibodashi area of Tokyo, Japan. It was renovated to its present form in 1958 at a cost of $750,000. The Kodokan has more than sixty rooms, including seven dojo. The main dojo has more than enough space for five hundred mats, with three smaller dojo of over a hundred mats. The facility also has showers, a weight room, and twenty dormitory rooms. There are also a library, a basement dining room, administrative offices, and large conference rooms.

What makes the dojo floor of the Kodokan unique?

The floor was constructed on large spring coils so that when hundreds of students are practicing their throws, the floor actually "gives" to help absorb the shock of the falling bodies.

What happened to the old Kodokan hall?

It now houses the Japan Karate Association and serves as its international headquarters.

Which U.S. President studied judo?

Theodore Roosevelt studied judo from Yoshiaki Yamashita, one of Jigoro Kano's foremost disciples.

Which noted movie star was also a judo black belt?

James Cagney.

Is there a Korean form of judo?

Yes; it's called yudo (*you*-doe). There is almost no difference between it and the Kodokan judo taught in Japan.

What is the first movement one learns in judo?

The all-important breakfalls, known technically as ukemi (oo-*kem*-ee). Obviously, this logical necessity is taught first because one cannot learn to throw an opponent, and especially to be thrown by an opponent, until the proper way to fall without injury is perfected.

How many different types of breakfalls are there in judo?

There are five breakfalls: forward, backward, left side, right side, and forward somersault.

What influence has Mel Bruno had on judo?

Emilio Bruno's influence on judo can be appropriately described in one word: profound. Bruno became the fifth American to earn a black belt in Kodokan judo when he received the honor personally from its founder, Jigoro Kano, in 1935. He subsequently became the first American to receive 5th- and 6th-degree black-belt ranks in judo. Bruno competed in the National AAU Judo Championships in 1939, finishing second at 158 pounds, and was scheduled to participate in the 1940 Olympics in Japan, which were canceled because of the impending war.

From 1937 to '41, Bruno served as a part-time judo instructor at the San Jose State College Police School. He formed the nation's first college judo team, and in 1940 he and the late Henry Stone of the University of California at Berkeley brought their teams together for the first intercollegiate judo competition in U.S. history. In 1944, Bruno introduced judo at Cornell University in Ithaca, New York.

In 1942, Bruno was recruited by former world heavyweight boxing champion Gene Tunney, then commander of the U.S. Navy's program on physical fitness, as the instructor in charge of combatives at the USN Physical Instructor Training School. In 1946, he was appointed to direct physical training and judo for the State of California Department of Corrections, overseeing the training of correctional officers in ten institutions.

In 1951, Bruno became supervisor of judo and combative measures for the United States Air Force Strategic Air Command. He initiated the establishment of Air Force classes for training at the Kodokan in Japan and arranged the Kodokan's team tour of the U.S. Air Force bases in the States in 1953. He received special commendation for his work in SAC from General Curtis LeMay, who was also one of Bruno's judo students.

In 1950, he arranged for the Kodokan to be the official representative of the U.S. Judo Black Belt Federation and the AAU (Amateur Athletic Union). He had already requested AAU recognition of judo. Approval was given unanimously and Bruno was appointed to develop the AAU judo program.

In 1955, he initiated the first judo tournament between the United States and Japan and was selected as coach of the AAU and Air Force teams. He served as coach of the U.S. judo teams, competing at both the 1958 World Judo Championships in Tokyo and the 1961 World Championships in Paris. In 1964, he prepared the Air Force Judo Team for the Olympic Tryouts. The team placed fourth, and two players made the Olympic team.

Emil Bruno has made films and written a multitude of training and administrative manuals in addition to all his earlier achievements. His overall devotion to and promotion of judo has been of inestimable effect.

What is Camp Olympus?

Camp Olympus, originated by all-time great judo competitor Jim Bregman, is the biggest judo camp on the East Coast. The camp operates for two weeks every summer, and Bregman has been instrumental in importing Europe's celebrated champions and instructors to conduct camp seminars and lectures. His guest instructors have included 1964 Olymic champion and all-time judo great Anton Geesink of Holland, and noted English judo author and trainer G. R. Gleason.

Why can't one wear a sweatsuit when practicing judo?

Because the fabric would not hold up to the tremendous strain of the pulling and twisting grasps of a partner. Such tugging is mandatory to execute most judo throws.

Has judo founder Jigoro Kano ever written a book on his art?

Yes. The book, entitled *Judo*, was written in 1937 and published by the Japan Board of Tourist Industry. It has been translated into English.

What is the name and function of the official national judo organization of the United States?

The Judo Black Belt Federation (JBBF), the only recognized judo body in America. The JBBF has the responsibility of supervising standards, examining students for black-belt rank, and publicizing and promoting sport judo.

Who is responsible for supervising college judo?

The National Collegiate Judo Association, recognized by the Judo Black Belt Federation, is responsible for the administration of judo at college and university levels.

Throwing techniques are one of the four major phases of judo training. Here Gene Le-Bell, former U.S. National champion, is being thrown by his student.

What are the three original purposes of judo as laid down by its founder, Jigoro Kano?

Judo is designed first and foremost as a system of physical training for the improvement of the body by emphasizing "big" muscle activity. Judo exerts a positive influence on strengthening the body and making it more physically efficient. Secondly, judo is designed as a competitive sport that is controlled by strict rules. Finally, it is meant to improve mental ability. By constant practice, an attitude of mind develops which greatly improves the degree of composure, and requires the use of imagination, reasoning, and judgment. This develops for the student a quick mind for making decisions and taking prompt action in normal activities of everyday life.

How many divisions are there in judo?

To simplify the study of judo it has been divided into four major parts: throwing techniques, nage waza (*naw*-gay *waw*-za); grappling techniques, katame waza (ka-*taw*-may *waw*-za); striking techniques, ate waza (*aw*-tay *waw*-za); and the resurrection techniques, kappo waza (*cop*-poh *waw*-za). The last two divisions are taught only to highly advanced students, so most of the training falls under the first two aspects.

How are major judo techniques divided?

nage waza (throwing techniques)

tachi waza
(standing throwing techniques)

sutemi waza
(sacrifice throwing techniques)

te waza (hand techniques)
koshi waza (loin or hip techniques)
ashi waza (foot or leg techniques)

ma sutemi waza (back sacrifice techniques)
yoko sutemi waza (side sacrifice techniques)

katame waza (grappling techniques)

tachi waza
(standing grappling techniques)

ne waza
(ground techniques)

shime waza (choking techniques)
kansetsu waza (joint-locking techniques)
osaekomi waza (holding or immobilization techniques)
shima waza (choking techniques)
kansetsu waza (joint-locking techniques)

ate waza (striking techniques)

ude waza (hand and arm techniques)
ashi waza (foot and leg techniques)

Roughly, how long does it take to advance from one belt to the next in judo?

If a student practices a minimum of two or three times per week in a recognized judo school it should take approximately the following:

Beginning and Intermediate

rokkyu (*row*-cue)—6th class	beginning
gokyu (*go*-cue)—5th class	5 to 8 months
yonkyu (*yawn*-cue)—4th class	8 to 12 months

Beginning and Intermediate (*Cont.*)

sankyu (*sawn*-cue)—3rd class	1 to 1½ years
nikyu (*knee*-cue)—2nd class	1½ to 2 years
ikkyu (*ee*-cue)—1st class	2 to 3 years

Black Belt

shodan (*show*-dawn)—1st rank	3 to 4 years
nidan (*knee*-dawn)—2nd rank	4 to 6 years
sandan (*sawn*-dawn)—3rd rank	6 to 8 years
yodan (*yoh*-dawn)—4th rank	9 years or more

Fifth-degree black belt and above are honorary.

How are judo rank examinations held?

A judo examination is generally composed of three stages. In the first stage, the candidate must demonstrate fundamentals such as falling, moving, and grasping, as well as throwing and grappling techniques. There is usually a contest in the second stage in which the candidate must exhibit his knowledge in free-fighting. Finally, the candidate may be asked questions about sport judo, history, and philosophy, among other technical questions.

What is the highest rank any one judo instructor can bestow?

According to the Judo Black Belt Federation, the body responsible for supervision of judo rank, a judo instructor can promote a student only up to sankyu, or third-class brown belt, after which examinations must be given by an officially appointed board of black belts. These boards meet periodically during the year for just this purpose.

What are the three primary methods of study in judo?

They are kata (*caught*-ah), the formal exercises or prearranged forms; randori (ran-*door*-ee), free exercise or sparring; and shiai (*she*-eye), or contests.

Does judo competition, like karate, have kata divisions?

Yes. Kata, the form of shadowboxing, has its own competitive division in judo, but is performed quite differently from the kata in karate or kung-fu. Judo kata are prearranged forms which demonstrate the various techniques in their own ideal form. There are nine judo kata, including forms of throwing, grappling, defense, antique forms, forms of gentleness, and theoretical forms. These forms or routines are in some ways like fixed gymnastic routines. They demonstrate judo techniques in the most beautiful, efficient, and interesting way. Unlike the kata of other martial arts, judo forms are always practiced with a partner.

Is judo an AAU sport?

Yes. Judo was accepted by the Amateur Athletic Union in 1953, when the first National AAU Judo Championships were held at San Jose State College. The AAU now has, in addition to senior men's judo competition, allotted form and fighting divisions for women, and Junior Olympic competition for boys below the age of seventeen.

Is judo in the Pan-American Games? Is it an Olympic sport?

Yes. Judo competition has been included in the Pan-American Games since 1963, when they were held in São Paulo, Brazil. In 1964, judo was officially entered into the Olympic Games in Tokyo.

Who controls international competition for American judo contestants?

The AAU. All athletes, including those on Pan-American and Olympic judo teams, must be certified amateurs by the AAU. The United States Olympic Judo Committee, under the constitution of the U.S. Olympic Committee, controls the selection of the Pan-American and Olympic judo teams.

Who were the first U.S. Olympic judo team members?

Lightweight Paul Maruyama of San Jose, California; middleweight Jim Bregman of Washington, D.C.; heavyweight George Harris, then of the U.S. Air Force; and openweight Ben Campbell of Sacramento, California. The Olympics were staged in Tokyo in 1964 when judo was first included.

Did any Americans place in the 1964 Olympic Games?

Yes. Jim Bregman won a bronze medal in the middleweight division. He was thus the first American ever to win a judo event in the Olympics.

Who was the first Olympic open champion?

Holland's Anton Geesink.

What is the governing body for judo in the Western Hemisphere?

The Pan-American Judo Union (PJU).

When and where were the first National AAU Judo Championships held?

At San Jose State College in California in 1963.

Which international judo organization is responsible for general supervision of world judo?

The International Judo Federation is the world's most powerful judo body. It is composed of member countries interested in planning international and Olympic judo competitions, and also serves as the supervisory body for standards of world judo.

What is the role of the Amateur Athletic Union (AAU) in U.S. judo?

Judo is recognized by the AAU as an official sport. The AAU protects the amateur status of all judo students under its jurisdiction in the United States. Largely through its efforts, judo has remained free from professionalism.

Can armlocks be used in judo?

Yes, but only by practitioners of brown-belt rank and above.

What is *Willow in the Wind?*

The name of an American newsletter for female judoka published in the mid-1960s.

What is the go kyo no waza?

Five stages of techniques developed by Jigoro Kano for teaching judo. Developed in 1896, the five stages are differentiated by their degree of difficulty. The go kyo was revised in 1920 by Dr. Kano and his associates at the Kodokan. It is used throughout the world as a basis for teaching judo.

What is nage no kata?

Known literally as "forms of throwing," it is the first kata, or form, which judo students are required to learn. Composed of fifteen overall throws, it includes hand, waist, and foot techniques, as well as sacrifice throws.

One of the hand techniques from nage-no-kata ("forms of throwing") includes the one-arm shoulder throw as seen here performed by two top-ranking judo men.

What is katame no kata?

Known literally as the "forms of holding," it is the second kata which judo students are required to master.

Are there many injuries in judo?

In a survey undertaken several years ago by the Medical Committee of the U.S. Judo Federation, it was reported that only seventy serious injuries and accidents occurred among 200,000 active judo players in the United States. This reflects the fact that judo is a relatively safe sport when properly taught and supervised.

How did Jigoro Kano use kata to make judo popular?

Kano realized that to have judo widely accepted in Japan it had to gain official government sanctioning. To achieve this, he appealed to the Ministry of Education. But before they would accept judo, Kano had to prove that it differed from jujutsu as an educational entity. One of the methods he used to convince them was a demonstration of the ju no kata (forms of gentleness). It thus brought judo into the educative sphere because the kata, when properly performed, results in a harmoniously developed, flexible, and strong body, as well as teaching the user the fundamental mechanics of judo.

Other Martial Arts and Weaponry

To some, the mention of martial arts immediately brings to mind the arts of karate, judo, and/or kung-fu. This association is reasonable, since these disciplines have become popular branches of the martial-arts family tree. But there are many lesser-known methods of fighting and self-defense, aikido and jujutsu among them, which seem to have received only cursory attention in the United States. Nevertheless, some of these arts attract large numbers of enthusiasts in their Asian homeland, and have to some extent spread elsewhere.

Weaponry, on the other hand, has been a topical subject ever since some caveman fashioned the first club from what was probably a tree limb. The Orient, steeped in mysticism for centuries, has evolved a class of weapons both strange and sophisticated. For instance, Japan's ninja clan were far ahead of their time in the field of weaponry. Their practices were so ingenious that the late Ian Fleming chose to include them and their methods as part of the story line in his James Bond adventure novel **You Only Live Twice.**

Because of the curious nature of this weaponry, and the fact that these instruments were invented by those who practiced secret, unorthodox systems of combat, the authors felt it oppropriate to combine the two subjects in one chapter.

What is aikido?

Aikido (eye-*key*-doe) is a Japanese method of self-defense which took root from the jujutsu style known as aiki-jutsu (eye-key-*jut*-sue). Aikido was founded by Morihei Uyeshiba in 1942 in Tokyo, Japan, and is based on nonresistance with an assailant. Although there are some striking techniques included, it is not principally considered a percussion art. Instead, an aikidoist attempts to use his opponent's forces against him by turning him around the aikidoist's center axis. It is therefore viewed as an art of pacifism and has no type of competition.

What is arnis de mano?

More prominently known as escrima (es-*cream*-a), arnis de mano is the most popular martial art in the Philippines. It is best noted for its use of two short sticks for combative purposes, but it also utilizes various other weapons as well as empty-hand techniques.

What is kendo?

Kendo (*ken*-doe) is the modern art of Japanese fencing performed with bamboo swords. Kendo enthusiasts don protective head, chest, and arm equipment in order to cushion the blows. The art is based on the development of only seven efficient blows and one thrusting technique. Literally, "kendo" means "way of the sword."

Where and when did kendo originate?

Kendo's history reaches back to the feudal days of Japan, when the sword was the major weapon carried by the Japanese warrior. As warfare decreased, the necessity to carry the sword decreased proportionately, so the Japanese began to practice shinai-geiko (shin-eye-*gay*-koh), training with a mock sword. By the late 1700s this was the only major use of the sword. As time passed, various masters added knowledge to the art of the sword, and eventually kendo developed. In 1909, the first organized kendo group in Japan was formed. It was called the University Kendo Federation. In 1928, the All-Japan Kendo Federation was founded, and it began to standardize the art, which, up to then, was practiced in hundreds of different manners.

What is the three-sectional staff?

The three-sectional staff is a wooden stave consisting of three distinct parts, with the end sections connected to the middle segment by metal rings. Its length varies but is usually 5 feet. The weapon was created by a Chinese emperor during the Sung Dynasty for use by his soldiers against adversaries carrying shields. The long-range capabilities of the three-sectional staff made it possible to flap an end around the soldier's shield to penetrate his defense. It was also used to

Eric Lee (right), one of America's most noted kung-fu practitioners, uses the three-sectional staff against an opponent wielding a spear.

upset a mounted soldier by tripping his horse and thus bringing the horseman down to fight on an equal level.

Is kick-boxing an American art?

Definitely not. Better known as Thai kick-boxing because of its native origin, it was once the hand-to-hand combat method used to supplement armed warfare in Thailand. Thai kick-boxing has now grown into an exciting sport and national pastime in its native country. From 1969–70, a form of kick-boxing was used competitively in the United States.

What is kwonpup?

Kwonpup (*quan*-pup) is an early Chinese method of unarmed combat which spread to and was popularized in Korea from 1147–1170. It was later developed into two advanced systems and is the earliest forerunner of tae kwon do, the most popular Korean martial art today. It was also known as kwonbop (*quan*-bop).

What is jujutsu?

This early Japanese hand-to-hand combative discipline applied to both armed and unarmed combat and was characterized by rudimentary kicking and striking, joint-locking, throwing, holding, choking, and the use of various weapons. It is the art from which both aikido and judo took root.

What is iaido?

Iaido (ee-*eye*-doe) is the modern art of drawing the samurai sword from its scabbard. Iaido stems from iai-jutsu (ee-eye-*jut*-sue), the classical method of swordsmanship based upon the perfection of the initial movement of the sword and the instant striking of an opponent.

What is the rokushakubo?

The rokushakubo (row-koo-sha-*koo*-bow) is a polelike hardwood weapon, usually 6 feet in length. Its use is closely related to the movements of the early Okinawa te (*tay*) systems.

What is the sai?

The sai (*sigh*) is a pronged swordlike truncheon which was developed and used by Okinawan farmers as an effective defense against various weapons and empty-hand attacks. When the Japanese occupied Okinawa and all weaponry was confiscated, the natives were forced to develop several self-defense weapons to defend against attacks by Japanese soldiers and marauders. The sai was specifically suited to counterattacks of the wooden staff or the samurai sword, though it was equally effective against empty-hand assaults. The sai is believed to have been derived from the pitchfork and is one of the five systematized weapons created by the early te developers of Okinawa.

What is wu shu?

Wu shu (*woo*-shoe), "war arts," is an encompassing terms for the Chinese martial arts. More recently, it has been called the unwarlike, self-expressive, and physical-fitness arts of the "new" Chinese society. For all intents and purposes, wu shu is basically kung-fu. Yet, through political influence, modern wu shu is considered more a means of physical conditioning than a type of fighting discipline.

The sai, held here by black belt Emil Farkas (right), was used by Okinawan farmers to defend themselves against various weapons such as the staff seen above.

Can tai chi chuan be used as a means of self-defense, or is it merely a form of exercise?

Tai chi chuan (tie-chee-*chwawn*) is widely practiced in China as well as in other parts of the world for its healthful benefits. However, it was created as a form of pugilism and has evolved to a form of calisthenic-type exercise. Tai chi chuan is one of the easiest martial arts to identify. It is characterized by deliberate, slow-motion movements that are continuous, circular, and rhythmic. Don't let its slow movements deceive you, though. Once speeded up for more practical purposes it obviously becomes an unquestionable self-defensive art, thus reflecting its pugilistic tradition.

How does sumo wrestling differ from American wrestling?

Sumo (*sue*-mow) is a basic Japanese form of unclad grappling in which the participants are of gigantic proportions. Some contestants weigh in at more than four hundred pounds. While American wrestling is conducted under a set of complex rules, sumo wrestling is quite simple. A victory is determined when the ground is met with any other part of the body than the feet. A victory in the American grappling art is reached when an opponent submits or is pinned for a predetermined period of time. Thus, American wrestling matches can last for prolonged periods, while a sumo contest, with much etiquette and tradition involved, can be completed in just a few seconds.

Is aikido related more to judo or to karate?

Aikido is related to both judo and karate in that it is an Oriental combative discipline and is based not only on the physical, but on the mental and spiritual as well. Aikido, however, is much more related to judo, since both require contact to be made with the trunk of the body. In addition, both arts stem from an earlier art, jujutsu. Nonetheless, aikido has not achieved status as a sport, while judo is a recognized Olympic sport.

What is the difference between bojutsu and jojutsu?

Bojutsu (bow-*jut*-sue) is the art of practicing with the long staff, which is generally 6 feet in length. Jojutsu (joe-*jut*-sue) is the art of the short stick, which is usually 2 to 3 feet long.

How was the sai developed?

Originally, the Okinawan sai or short sword was formed of two components, the curved prong section and the main stem. These separate parts were then pounded into a single unit, using a process similar to that employed by Japanese swordsmiths. Approximately a century ago, a less primitive method of making the sai was developed. A finished sai was laid in sand to cast an indentation. When the sai was removed, molten lead was poured into the resulting cavity. Once the lead cooled and hardened, rough edges were ground and the finished instrument was polished.

How did the Okinawans conceal their weapons?

During the Japanese occupation of Okinawa some 350 years ago, invading warlords prohibited the use of ordinary weapons such as the sword or spear. So, to protect themselves from bandits and Japanese marauders, the ingenious Okinawans turned to karate and kobudo (Koh-*boo*-doe), the way of weapons. Most of the kobudo instruments were farm implements converted to effective protective devices. For instance, the sai or short, pronged sword was dragged through the soil by one peasant, while another would plant seed in the resulting furrow. On the approach of a marauding samurai warrior, the sai doubled as a weapon with which the farmer could counter both empty-hand and weapons attacks.

What is kobudo?

Kobudo (koh-*boo*-doe), "weapons way," is the art of Okinawan weaponry practiced in conjunction with various styles of karate in their advanced stages.

Some of the various weapons used in the Oriental martial arts are: (1) yari (spear); (2) snake spear; (3) trident; (4) single sword; (5) bokken (wooden sword); (6) nunte; (7) tonfa; (8) sai; (9) jutte (10) kama (sickle); (11) nine-ring sword; (12) wakizashi; (13) straight sword; (14) katana; (15) shinai; (16) nunchaku; (17) naginata; and (18) shuriken (stars).

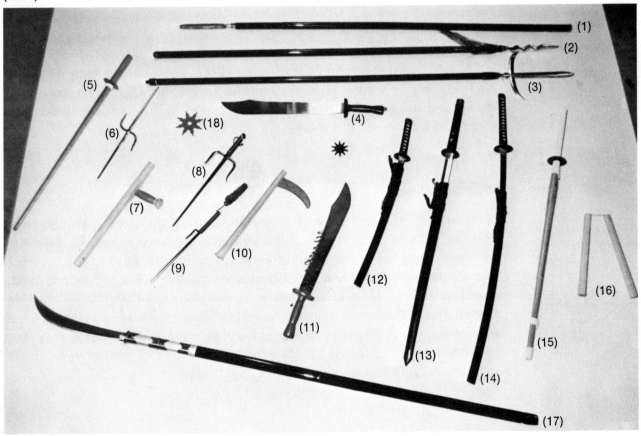

The nunchaku (nun-*chaw*-ka), bo (*bow*), sai (*sigh*), kama (*kah*-ma), tonfa (*tawn*-fa), and surushin (sue-*rue*-shin) are some weapons which were improvised from farm instruments by Okinawans. The spike or shuriken (sure-*ee*-ken) and manrikigusari (man-ree-key-gu-*saw*-ree) or chain and sickle, among several other weapons which stemmed from Japan, are also considered authentic weapons arts.

How was the sai employed as a weapon?

The sai originally was capable of killing or maiming an enemy with a blow to the back of the neck or a thrust to the throat or eyes. Usually, the Okinawan farmer used two sai, one for each hand, and concealed a third inside his obi (*oh*-bee) or belt. The sai would first be used to counter an attack by trapping an attacker's bare hand or weapon between the main stem and the prongs. Then, it was used to physically disable the opponent in a variety of fashions. Sometimes, the Okinawans would first draw the sai from their belt and attempt to subdue an adversary by pinning his foot to the ground with the sharp point of the sai.

Today, the sharp points of the sai have been blunted and rounded for use as an artistic, cultural form in modern martial-arts practices. It no longer serves as a weapon for mortal combat.

How was the sai used in Japan?

The Japanese police found the sai quite effective when making arrests by using it against the various pressure points of the criminals they apprehended. It was around this time that one prong was removed at the handle and the name was changed to the jutte (*jew*-tay).

What is pankration?

Pankration, meaning "game of all powers," is an early Greek sport developed as a combination of the even earlier forms of Greek boxing and wrestling. Any technique except eye-gouging and biting was permitted. Kicking was common, and statues exist that show practitioners completing what in modern karate would be called a front kick. While most historians seem content to trace the martial arts to the Indian vajramushti system, since any further investigation is hampered by lack of evidence, one thing that can be noted, however, is that pankration and Pyrrhic both antedate the Indian statues depicting temple guards in poses similar to those used in latter-day fighting arts.

How was the sai introduced to America?

During the mid-1960s, Americans became increasingly aware of its existence through demonstrations at karate tournaments. Robert Trias of Arizona and Fumio Demura of California were two of its earliest proponents. Later, U.S. karate promoters instituted a separate division for weapons competition when the practice of weaponry became widespread.

What are the five major weapons systems of Okinawan karate?

The five systematized weapons which have been structured into an organized teaching method are the bo, sai, nunchaku, kama, and tonfa. These are the primary weapons taught in conjunction with advanced stages of Okinawan and Japanese karate.

What is jeet kune do?

Jeet kune do, or "way of the intercepting fist," is the late Bruce Lee's personal style of combat, now carried on principally by his protégé Dan Inosanto of Torrance, California. Jeet kune do has been defined as a collection of basic mental and physical concepts, observations of combat maneuvers, and philosophies of attitude. As the definition relates, jeet kune do was anything but traditional.

Technically, there is no such thing as jeet kune do as defined and compared to other styles of the martial arts. While JKD did exist in one form as practiced by its founder, it no longer exists in that form. Even Lee's form differed on occasion, and this was his intention. The reasoning is simple if one is familiar with Lee's philosophy. He believed that the martial arts as illustrated by styles, patterns, and doctrines could never be more important than the individual practicing them. He therefore made JKD a personal experience expressed by a combination of *all* the martial arts, including Western boxing.

The practice of jeet kune do stresses the person, not the style. Whereas other forms of the martial arts are models of ancient traditions, JKD is a mirror image of the practitioner, who gleans the best from the established arts and incorporates them to fit his own physical and spiritual being.

The only prerequisites for jeet kune do are fluid motion and adaptability. This means that punches, kicks, and throws must go through the line of attack and not just to it. It might best be described as the *modern* martial art.

What is the nunte?

The nunte (*nun*-tay) is a weapon similar in shape and size to the sai except that one prong points toward the bearer and the other projects outward. The central shaft extends on both ends beyond the point where the prongs intersect. There is another version of the nunte used by early-twentieth-century Japanese policemen. This version bore only one prong and was called the jutte (*jew*-tay). The two-pronged nunte is usually placed on the end of the bo or long staff, thus making it a long-range weapon.

What is the nunchaku?

The nunchaku (nun-*chaw*-koo) is a universally hinged wooden flail which was converted into an effective weapons art by Okinawan farmers some 350 years ago. Basically, the nunchaku consists of two sticks connected by rope, nylon cord, or chain. There are many varieties now on the market, even though the weapon has been outlawed in numerous states.

The nunchaku is considered one of the simple yet dangerous weapons. "The nunchaku is a versatile device," *Newsweek* reported. "When the connecting cord is wrapped around a victim's neck, the two sticks give even a weak assailant enough leverage to throttle his foe. When one stick is held in the hand, the other can be swung with fearsome speed and power." The nunchaku is said to be able to generate 1,600 pounds of pressure at the point of impact. However, some human bones when struck require only about 8½ pounds of pressure to break.

Because of his use of nunchaku in a number of his films, Bruce Lee popularized the weapon overnight.

Why was the nunchaku developed?

Principally, as a tool to flail grain. Okinawan farmers then systematized it for use as a weapon during the Japanese occupation of the sixteenth century. Today, the weapon, like many others, holds wide appeal among martial artists, who retain its practice as part of their cultural and traditional karate training.

What is bando?

Bando (*ban*-doe) is a system of fighting practiced in Burma. It consists of various karate-related techniques of striking with the hands and feet, and blocking and countering. While the art appears to have some Chinese influence, it nonetheless is said to be native. Bando was brought to the United States by Dr. Maung Gyi of Athens, Ohio.

What is the tonfa?

The tonfa (*tawn*-fa), also known as the tui-fa (*twee*-fa), meaning "handle," is another of the farming implements converted to a weapon by Okinawan farmers. It was primarily used as a handle for a millstone. The weapon has a short handle for grasping, connected to a perpendicular handle. The weapon is generally held with the large handle running outside the forearm up past the elbow. It is used by thrusting, and both vertical and horizontal rotation.

What is sambo?

Sambo (*sam*-bow) is the Russian form of wrestling similar to judo. It is so closely related, in fact, that it has been included by the Russians as a part of the training for their international judo competitors. For this reason, it is not unusual to see a sambo player pitted against a judo opponent in open competition.

Are there different styles of jujutsu?

Much like any other Oriental combative discipline, jujutsu has its major and minor subdivisions.

How is the tonfa used?

Practitioners of the tonfa use the instrument for thrusting techniques as well as both horizontal and vertical applications. It is an extremely difficult weapon to employ, since the grips do not have a swivel hinge upon which to rotate their perpendicular counterparts. Thus, one using the weapon has to learn to ease his grip while it is swinging free, while tightening his grip upon contact with any target. Through this practice, the tonfa can improve coordination, dexterity, and the ability to focus, an important factor used in the empty-hand stage of karate.

Where did the kama originate?

The kama (*kah*-ma) or sickle was a simple instrument employed by Okinawan farmers. Its razor-sharp edge made the cutting of grain an easier chore. The sickle was an obvious convert to the weapons family, since the Japanese occupational forces did not forbid the farmer to use it in the fields in the course of his everyday work. But when the farmer faced a skilled samurai swordsman in mortal combat it became apparent that the short-range effectiveness of the weapon was a distinct disadvantage when used against a longer sword. So the farmers later renovated the kama by attaching a cord to its handle. By grasping the end of the cord, they could produce long-range as well as short-range results. They were also able to elaborate on the movements of the kama, and it came to be employed with the rotating methods more familiar to the nunchaku.

What is the bo?

The bo (*bow*) is a wooden stave generally about 6 feet in length. The long-range weapon is one of the five systematized weapons used by the early te developers in Okinawa.

Which is the oldest style of jujutsu?

Many historians acknowledge the Takenouchi school as the oldest branch of jujutsu. It was founded by Hisamoni Takenouchi in the fifteenth century.

What is the quando?

A weapon indigenous to kung-fu training, the quando (*quan*-doe) is a long heavy staff with an enormous, vicious-looking blade on one end and a sharp point on the other. Its weight and bulk are useful in building strength and a capability of responding to a wide variety of situations. The quando forms allegedly develop the body evenly so that no part is ever stronger or out of proportion to another.

What is the kung-fu chain?

The chain is only one of many weapons of the kung-fu arsenal. Composed of various lengths, it is whipped around the body at terrific speeds, its intricate revolutions demanding a flexible wrist and a good eye for distancing. A highly difficult weapon to master, it teaches the student how to control his momentum lest he suffer the consequences of having the vicious chain boomerang with alarming force and speed.

What is the double-edged sword?

It is considered the most difficult weapon to master in kung-fu. The double-edged sword is wielded in a relaxed manner, gently moved in small circles with increasing subtlety. When performed properly it amounts almost to a meditative experience to heighten the student's awareness.

Why do kung-fu advocates practice weaponry?

Training in the use of a wide variety of weapons has always been required in reputable kung-fu schools. China's long history of violent warfare further increased the need for weapons training. During these lawless periods, highwaymen and pirates roamed land and sea, plundering just about anything they came across. These predators were always armed, and a kung-fu man who relied merely on hand techniques was either a great master or a fool.

Also, a master was continually being challenged to maintain his reputation. The most serious challenges came from other masters eager to prove the superiority of their kung-fu system. If a challenger defeated a reigning master he would often inherit much of the defeated master's school. This was very often a lucrative proposition, so challenges were commonplace and frequently called for the use of weaponry. A kung-fu practitioner thus had to be as proficient with weaponry as he was in unarmed combat. Weaponry is still used today as part of tradition and is viewed as a very valuable method of enhancing unarmed techniques.

Martial Arts Personalities

This book would be incomplete if it didn't pay homage to some of the individuals who have helped make the martial arts the important part of the American scene that they have become. This chapter introduces personalities whose professions range from karate instructor to college professor, from sports star to minister. It provides a cross section of the type of people who have devoted their energies to the martial arts, and it explains the substantial contributions they have made. Both the reader new to the martial arts and the longtime fan will benefit from the facts the authors have included—facts to once and for all set the record straight as to who did what, and when and where it happened.

Who introduced karate to America?

There are disputes over who was really the pioneer of karate in the United States. Discounting Hawaii, the earliest known practitioner of the martial arts in America is Robert Trias of Phoenix, Arizona. Trias opened the first karate dojo (gym) in 1946. He formed the first karate organization in the United States, which he called the United States Karate Association, in 1948.

Three other early pioneers who were also instrumental in introducing America to the martial arts are Ed Parker of Los Angeles, who opened his first school in Utah in 1954; Tsutomu Ohshima of Los Angeles, who opened a school in 1955; and Jhoon Rhee of Washington, D.C., who began his school in Texas in 1956 while attending San Marcos Southwest Texas State College.

Which famous judo champion publicly defeated a boxer?

Judo champion and celebrated wrestler Gene LeBell accepted a public challenge in 1963 to appear as a judo/karate fighter against a boxer in a special bout to the knockout in Salt Lake City, Utah. LeBell earned a few thousand dollars by rendering unconscious world-rated lightheavyweight boxer Milo Savage in two rounds. LeBell, now retired, spends most of his time announcing and promoting wrestling bouts at the notorious Olympic Auditorium in Los Angeles.

Which famous karate master killed bulls with his bare hands?

Japan's Mas Oyama claims to have battled fifty-two bulls in his lifetime. According to further reports, he severed the horns from forty-eight of them and has killed three others with one powerful blow. Now in his fifties, Oyama no longer engages in such sensational feats. Nonetheless, his deeds are a matter of legend and continue to be discussed in karate circles throughout the world. With all due

World-famous karate instructor Mas Oyama (left) discusses the martial arts with former James Bond Sean Connery during the filming of *You Only Live Twice.* At right is noted author Donn Draeger.

respect to animal lovers, the three bulls he killed were marked for slaughter that same day.

Tadashi Yamashita is one of the most celebrated weapons performers in the United States. Is he Okinawan or Japanese?

Yamashita, who has thrilled audiences coast to coast with his daring display of Okinawan weaponry, is Japanese. Unlike most of his contemporaries, he studied in both Japan and Okinawa before coming to the United States.

Some observers claim Hollywood's Eric Lee is the most suitable candidate to follow in the footsteps of the late Bruce Lee. Has he done any film work?

Eric Lee, who is known as the "king of kata" for his fantastic demonstrations of form, has done no films to date. However, his agent claims he is being considered for a starring role opposite former James Bond George Lazenby. The film is scheduled to begin shooting sometime in 1977. Locations are India and Los Angeles.

Still others claim Eric's sifu (instructor), Al Dacascos, is the most suitable candidate to take over Lee's throne. Himself an aspiring actor, Dacascos was given serious consideration to play the starring role in the proposed film *Bruce Lee: His Life and Legend.*

Is there a "new" Bruce Lee?

There may be someone playing the role of Bruce Lee, but there has been no clear-cut successor to his throne. In late 1975, Warner Bros., makers of *Enter the Dragon,* signed Alex Kwok to play the lead role in the proposed film *Bruce Lee: His Life and Legend.* The Chinese-Canadian, who was to be known by the stage name Alex Kwon, was formerly rated the number-one form competitor in American tournament competition by *Professional Karate Magazine.* But Warner's option to do the film expired in January 1976, and, according to reports, First Artists, the company owned by superstars Paul Newman, Steve McQueen, Barbra Streisand, Sidney Poitier, and Dustin Hoffman, picked up the option.

What is unique about the Urquidez family?

The dynamic Urquidez clan is one of the few existing families whose six members hold a karate black belt. Arnold, the second-eldest brother, coaches the other five members. Benny is the most famous, having won more money in 1975 than any other full-contact fighter in the United States. Sister Lidia was a former women's sparring champion. The other brothers, Smiley, Armando, and Ruben, are all known as seasoned fighters and/or periodic form champions. Even Lidia's husband, Blinky Rodriquez, and cousin Manuel are veteran black belts. They prove that the family that kicks together sticks together.

Who is known as "The Cat"?

Gogen Yamaguchi, the international leader of the goju-ryu style of karate, was nicknamed "The Cat" because of certain unique feats of skill he was capable of performing, such as jumping in the air and kicking in three directions before landing, catching arrows shot at him, and catching the blade of a samurai sword.

What is Mas Oyama's real name?

Oyama's real name is Young-I Choi; he is of Korean ancestry.

Who heads the Japan Karate Association?

The JKA, one of the world's largest karate organizations, is run by Masatoshi Nakayama of Japan.

Which famous karate instructor heads the largest kenpo association in the United States?

California's Ed Parker, one of the early pioneers of karate in America, probably runs the largest kenpo organization in the States. His International Kenpo Karate Association (IKKA) was started back in the late 1950s, and now boasts members throughout the world. Parker teaches a modified brand of the traditional style which is more commonly known as American kenpo.

Does Jhoon Rhee teach his own personal style of karate?

Jhoon Rhee of Washington, D.C., is known as the "father of American tae kwon do," having introduced the Korean discipline to the United States in 1956. At the beginning of 1975, however, Rhee completely modified his teaching methods, simply calling his new style the "Jhoon Rhee System." He revolutionized his instruction in his chain of thirty studios to include performing kata to music, and training with a more realistic approach to actual fighting. Rhee also applied his knowledge of mechanics—speed, power, statics, dynamics—learned at the University of Texas to his karate teaching principles to achieve maximum body power when executing karate techniques.

At what age did Joe Lewis begin studying karate?

Joe Lewis took up karate in May 1964 at the age of twenty. His early training came under the guidance of Eizo Shimabuku on the island of Okinawa, where Lewis was stationed with the U.S. Marine Corps. One of only four fighters to have competed successfully for more than a decade, Lewis is now the world professional heavyweight champion. Photographs of his early training still hang in the dojo of Shimabuku.

Who was Chuck Norris' instructor?

Jae Chul Shin, who first taught in Korea, then later opened a school in New Jersey, taught Norris, one of the big-three all-time karate champions of the 1960s.

Where did Ed Parker receive his early training?

The American kenpo pioneer received most of his training in Hawaii from William K. S. Chow.

Who was Count Dante?

The late Count Dante's real name was John Keehan. Before his startling death in 1975 at age thirty-six from a blood clot brought on by an ulcer, Keehan stood out as one of the most controversial and colorful characters in American martial-arts history. Keehan was one of the early pioneers of the United States Karate Association and was instrumental in establishing many USKA schools throughout the Midwest. Though he was known as a teacher, Keehan's real forte was promoting. He would do almost anything to promote karate. He once walked down State Street in Chicago accompanied by a bull, claiming he was going to kill it with a karate blow at one of his many tournament presentations. He, along with USKA president Robert Trias, was also responsible for promoting the first major open karate tournament in the United States, the World Championships in Chicago in 1963. This particular event evolved into the USKA Grand Nationals, one of the largest elimination events in contemporary sport karate.

For reasons undisclosed, Keehan violently altered his martial-arts philosophy in 1966. He changed his name to Count Dante, a name which appeared frequently

Joe Lewis, one of the all-time great karate fighters, has now retired from active competition to pursue a full-time acting career. Lewis fought in the karate ring for more than a decade.

in his mail-order ads for his controversial book, *Dim Mak, the Death Touch*. About this time, Dante had a dispute with his employer, Gene Wyka, and allegedly taped a dynamite cap to a Wyka-owned dojo window. Dante was arrested immediately. The whole affair seems to have been blown out of proportion by the press, as there were numerous dynamiting incidents taking place in Chicago in those days that actually had nothing to do with karate or with Dante. He continued to find himself in difficult positions, however, as he soon afterward raided a competitor's karate studio. A bloody fight ensued and Jim Koncevic, one of karate's most prominent Midwest instructors of the period, was stabbed and killed with a sword.

Dante also claimed that he was involved in "death matches" in the Orient and the United States, though no documented records exist to substantiate his claims. Dante held a bare-knuckle fight-to-the-knockout tournament on August 1, 1967, the first full-contact event in American sport karate. It was called the World Federation of Fighting Arts Championships. Merely a handful of contestants showed up to compete, because a prominent karate magazine openly opposed the event, and since karate tournaments were still noncontact, the strict traditionalists of the period refused to get involved. One of Dante's students, Vic Reither of Addison, Illinois, was the victor.

Dante used his own organization to help promote mail-order sales of his book. He claimed to have been crowned "the world's deadliest fighting master by the World Federation of Fighting Arts." Since he was the president of the federation, he obviously bestowed the title on himself. Since his death, his followers have allegedly squabbled over who should take his place as the "world's deadliest fighting master."

Which infamous karate instructor was also a hairdresser?

Count Dante, or John Keehan, was a hairdresser by profession. He was once featured in a *National Enquirer* cover story entitled, "The World's Deadliest Fighter Is a Hairdresser."

From whom did Jim Kelly study karate?

The actor/martial artist started training in karate under the guidance of Indiana's Parker Shelton, who at the time owned a studio in Tennessee. After moving to California, Kelly took up Okinawa-te with Gordon Doversola.

What style of karate does Jim Kelly practice?

Self-admittedly, he practices the "Jim Kelly Method," a mixed style of un-

Seen here with Bob Wall, Jim Kelly (left), one of the few martial artists to have become motion-picture celebrities, reached stardom for his role in *Enter the Dragon,* starring the late Bruce Lee.

orthodox karate combinations. He also claims to teach his style only to black belts and celebrities who can pay his minimum rate of $100 per hour.

Who is the highest-paid karate instructor in America?

Since the death of Bruce Lee, *Enter the Dragon* co-star Bob Wall claims to be the highest-paid instructor. Teacher of many noted celebrities, both screen stars and entertainers, Wall charges as much as $200 per hour for private instruction. Wall's long-time friend and karate veteran Pat Johnson charges a minimum of $75 an hour for his private instruction. Johnson and actor Jim Kelly probably rank right below Wall for the highest fees charged.

Has veteran karate instructor Pat Johnson done any film work?

The former karate champion has done bit parts in numerous films, as well as working in the capacity of choreographer for fight scenes. Johnson made his acting debut in Bruce Lee's *Enter the Dragon* in 1973. To date, he has appeared in *Golden Needles* with Joe Don Baker and Burgess Meredith, and in *Black Belt Jones* with Jim Kelly. He later served as choreographer for *The Ultimate Warrior*, starring Yul Brynner and Max Von Sidow, and *Hot Potato*, again starring Jim Kelly. Johnson has been appointed as stunt coordinator for *Bruce Lee: His Life and Legend*, which, if it does move into production, will star Chinese-Canadian Alex Kwon in the lead role. In addition, Johnson has penned two scripts for future production by First Artists.

Does Jerry Smith teach karate to celebrities?

Although he is best known for his proficiency as a full-contact karate coach for professional fighters, the former regional karate champion also teaches self-defense to numerous black stars. Among his students are Gloria Hendry, Bernie Casey, pro basketball stars Sidney Wicks and Curtis Rowe, and pro football player Bob Geddes. Smith has also done personal security work with entertainers Stevie Wonder, Smokie Robinson, Diana Ross, and the Temptations.

Who did Aaron Banks receive his black belt from?

New York's premier promoter started his training with John Kuhl, an advocate of "combatu karate." However, Banks reportedly didn't care for the style because Kuhl failed to teach forms. Banks switched to goju-ryu karate, where he received his black belt from John Slocum.

Who is Peter Urban?

Now of New Jersey, Peter Urban is one of the founders of karate on the East Coast. Following his martial-arts studies in the Orient, where he was taught by such celebrated instructors as Japan's Gogen "The Cat" Yamaguchi, Urban came to America in 1960 and settled in New York City. After amassing a large following, Urban modified his traditional goju-ryu style, calling it American goju-ryu. Before his recent retirement, he trained a multitude of students who have in turn become noted East Coast practitioners.

Which noted American karate pioneer is a direct student of Gichin Funakoshi, the "father of modern karate?"

Tsutomu Ohshima is a direct student of Funakoshi's. He introduced his shoto-kan style to the United States in 1955 when he settled in Los Angeles. Ohshima also introduced karate tournaments to the United States when he promoted the Neisei Week Karate Championships in 1958. Years after the death of Funakoshi, Ohshima translated his massive manuscripts into the English-language book *Karate-Do Kyohan: The Master's Textbook*. The book has since become a best seller in its field.

Who is the "father of Canadian karate"?

Mas Tsuroka. He opened the first public karate school in the early 1960s in Toronto, Canada. A student of Dr. Tsuyoshi Chitose, the founder of Chito-ryu karate, Tsuroka was the first karate promoter to hold a major tournament in Canada, the Canadian Karate Championships in 1962. Since his modest beginnings, Tsuroka has turned out hundreds of black belts who have spread karate all over Canada.

How did karate pioneer Dan Ivan and Fumio Demura get together?

Dan Ivan returned to the United States after serving in the Armed Forces and studying several martial arts in the Orient after World War II. Ivan established a karate school in Orange County, California, and in 1965 brought Fumio Demura to the United States from Japan, where Ivan had earlier met and trained with him. As partners, they have since established twenty additional karate schools and have been active in promoting karate to non-practitioners of the martial arts through thousands of demonstrations. They have been particularly praised for their daily karate exhibitions for many years at the now defunct Japanese Village amusement park, and more recently, at Benihana's in the Las Vegas Hilton Hotel.

Which famous karate pioneer served as an undercover agent after World War II?

California's Dan Ivan was a former member of the CID of the American occupational forces in Japan from 1948 to 1956. Ivan has recently published a novel, *Tokyo Undercover*, based on his own true experiences as an undercover agent. The novel includes many actual incidents in which Ivan was forced to use his martial-arts expertise.

Fumio Demura (left), famous for his demonstrations at California's Japanese Village, displays the type of superior form and control which has thrilled thousands of tourists.

Are there any famous East Coast karate instructors who are also known for their work as undercover agents?

There are two individuals whose undercover work as narcotics agents has brought them notoriety—New York's Frank Ruiz and New Jersey's Don Nagel. Both East Coast karate instructors underwent some rather hair-raising experiences in the line of undercover duty. Nagel continues his work today as a full-time profession. Following a tragic accident unrelated to his undercover work which nearly crippled him for life, Ruiz has moved into other professions, including stunt choreography for motion pictures.

Which noted Midwest karate instructor was killed in an actual dojo war during the 1960s?

Chicago's Jim Koncevic was killed in a fracas with the late Count Dante when Dante's students, accompanied by their leader, raided a competitor's karate school. Koncevic, a close friend and student of Dante's, was slain in the resultant battle with the competitor's students. Dante escaped without injury.

Which two famous American karatemen were born in Hawaii?

Both Mike Stone and Ed Parker were born and raised in Hawaii. Parker received his martial-arts training there under Professor William K. S. Chow, while Stone was introduced to karate in 1963 during his tour of duty with the U.S. Army at Fort Chaffee, Arkansas.

Who was Mike Stone's first instructor?

Herbert Peters, an Army staff sergeant and karate instructor, taught Mike Stone at Fort Chaffee, Arkansas. Following his discharge, Peters returned to his home state of Hawaii. Stone went on to become one of karate's most lauded champions of the 1960s.

Who was Willie Norris?

Willie was the brother of legendary fighter Chuck Norris. A promising tournament star, Willie was tragically killed in Korea while serving in the U.S. Air Force.

What was Pat Wyatt's claim to fame?

Chicago's Pat Wyatt had a reputation for outspokenness and honesty second to none. Besides being straightforward, Wyatt developed many of the organizational and registrational systems used in elimination-type karate tournaments today. Though he was never given credit, he had engineered numerous plans that were designed to provide a more organized tournament for both players and promoters by speeding up the registration and elimination processes. He was an exacting instructor; his students accumulated more than five hundred competition trophies from 1969 to 1974. Wyatt's record in 1971 earned him the United States Karate Association's prestigious "Coach of the Year" award. He was nominated and had placed in the top three positions for that same honor for four consecutive years since 1967 before finally winning it.

On a tragic Monday morning while working out with karate veteran Glenn Keeney, his friend from Anderson, Indiana, Wyatt complained of feeling tired and sat down to rest. He was suddenly stricken with a heart attack, and he died shortly afterward, at age thirty-two. His passing left the Midwest karate community in deep grief.

Hungarian-born Alex Sternberg (right), besides being a high-ranking black belt, is also an ordained rabbi. He has gained distinction in karate as one of the foremost kata competitors on a national level.

What unfortunate incident befell New York's Frank Ruiz in 1970?

In July 1970, Ruiz was changing a tire on the Brooklyn-Queens Expressway when he was struck by a car traveling at eighty miles per hour. Because of his multiple and critical injuries, doctors predicted he would not live, and that if he did, he would never walk again without crutches. Ruiz spent one week in a coma and eight months in a hospital, and underwent several operations on his leg. Upon his release in 1971, he immediately went back to teaching karate and giving demonstrations—on crutches. While demonstrating in Florida, he snapped the pins supporting his leg and had to endure yet another operation. In 1974, he discarded his crutches and once again walked normally. He has since continued teaching his craft, and has appeared in four movies as an actor and technical adviser for martial-arts fight scenes.

Where did Jeff Smith begin studying karate?

The lightheavyweight champion of the world initiated his karate training in 1966 at Texas A&M College. He received his black belt from Jhoon Rhee in 1969, and he started teaching karate in Washington, D.C., one year later. Smith now holds the position of chief instructor of the Jhoon Rhee Institutes and marketing manager of Jhoon Rhee's Safe-T Equipment Co.

For what feat is Professor Rodney Sacharnowski noted?

Sacharnowski performs one of the most unusual and dangerous demonstrations in the martial arts. He and his advanced students invite people from the audience to strike them with full force on nearly every part of the body, including the neck, groin, and temple. Participants may use any punch or kick of their choice. Sacharnowski claims that by using ki, or inner strength, he and his protégés are able to absorb these blows without injury. They are still numbered among the living, and furthermore, there are no reports of their having been wounded in action, an obvious credit to their strange powers.

What makes New York's Alex Sternberg unique among martial artists?

Sternberg, an immigrant from Hungary, is an ordained rabbi. He was once the chief instructor for the Jewish Defense League, a militant Jewish group, and has been arrested but never convicted on several occasions. His most positive accomplishment is his work in getting karate accepted as part of the Jewish Olympics, which will include karate beginning in 1977.

Who is considered the principal karate historian in the United States?

San Francisco's Richard Kim has long been considered the principal authority on karate's history and traditions. A long-time columnist for *Karate Illustrated Magazine,* Kim also wrote the book *The Weaponless Warriors: An Informal History of Okinawan Karate,* and was responsible for editing the Japanese entries in the first four-language *Encyclopedia of the Martial Arts.*

Who is considered the principal kung-fu historian in the United States?

Dr. William C. C. Hu of New York is probably best recognized in this capacity. Dr. Hu, a college professor, has contributed historical articles on the subject of kung-fu to *Black Belt Magazine* since as far back as the early 1960s, when the publication first came into existence. He has since been collecting data to write a comprehensive book on the subject.

Which famous Japanese karate instructor makes his home in Louisiana?

Takayuki Mikami, a former All-Japan karate champion and co-chief referee of the 1974 World Professional Karate Championships, operates four schools out of Louisiana. He makes his home in Metairie.

How did Ed Parker get his start in California?

Aside from opening a dojo in Pasadena on his own, Parker received additional help from Terry Robinson. Robinson, who was running the Beverly Hills Health Club and teaching physical fitness to stars such as Mario Lanza, permitted Parker to stage a demonstration of karate there. Parker was so impressive that several prominent entertainers immediately began taking lessons from him.

Which college professor is also a noted full-contact fighter?

Dr. Maung Gyi, a communications and psychology Ph.D. and a University of Ohio faculty member, has fought ninety-six full-contact bouts since 1950. The chief instructor of the American Bando Association, Dr. Gyi is still fighting virtually every weekend when he teaches bando classes. He has competed under both Asian and Western systems of fighting, and all of his matches have ended in knockouts. His current record stands at sixty-three wins and thirty-three losses.

Who are some noted martial-arts pioneers who received their early training in the Armed Forces?

The most famous martial artist to come out of the Air Force was Chuck Norris. However, the most notable influence has come from the Marines, since many of them were stationed in the Orient after World War II. They include Steve Armstrong, Joe Lewis, Steve Sanders, Glenn Premru, and Jerry Smith, among numerous others. Out of the Army came karatemen Dan Ivan, Mike Anderson, and Mike Stone, and judokas Paul Mariyama and Sgt. George Harris.

Which Methodist minister became a noted kung-fu author?

Best known for his work as a writer, Stockton's Leo Fong has published two books, *Sil Lum Kung-Fu* and *Choy Lay Fut Kung-Fu,* both of which are in their fifth printing, and he is the co-author of *Power Training in Kung-Fu and Karate.* During his years as a Methodist minister, Fong promoted the martial arts as a vehicle of communication with delinquent youths, teaching them the value of karate and kung-fu for development of a strong self-image.

What is Dan Inosanto's full-time profession?

The Bruce Lee protégé works as a physical-education instructor at a junior high school near his martial-arts studio in Carson, California.

What child received a black belt at age nine?

Young Philip Paley of Los Angeles, perhaps the most famous of the growing number of black-belt-ranked adolescents, received his promotion from Chuck Norris at age nine. Paley then appeared on several national TV shows with his instructor.

Who was known for cutting watermelons off the stomachs of students in his unique karate and weapons demonstrations?

Tadashi Yamashita, now of Tustin, California, gained national acclaim with his unique and sometimes blood-curdling weapons demos. He was best known for using a razor-sharp samurai sword to cut a watermelon in half while it was supported on the stomach of a supine student. And he performed the feat only after blindfolding himself!

Which famous martial artist performs a demonstration with the use of a board of nails?

New York's exciting showman Hidy Ochiai. For the finale of his unusual exhibition he lies on a sharp bed of nails and permits an assistant to smash, with a sledge hammer, several concrete slabs supported on his stomach. Ochiai has performed his demo both here and abroad, and he seldom fails to gain wild and enthusiastic ovations wherever he appears. When he is not demonstrating his art, Ochiai competes successfully in karate form competition. In 1975, he was rated America's number-one kata champion five consecutive times.

What style does Moses Powell teach?

The New York instructor teaches a little-known brand of jujutsu called vee-jitsu.

Who is famous for his impersonation of Bruce Lee?

New York's William Louie has become widely known for his "Tribute to Bruce Lee," an exciting demonstration he performs with the help of his students. In his act, Louie has captured to perfection the movements, facial expressions, and unique screams of the late martial-arts movie idol. Louie seldom fails to draw standing ovations wherever he performs.

Who founded the wado-ryu style of karate?

Hironori Otsuka founded this popular Japanese style, basing it on earlier jujutsu and karate systems. Wado-ryu, or "the way of peace," is one of the four major styles of Japanese karate.

Who introduced shito-ryu karate to Japan?

Okinawan Kenwa Mabuni founded shito-ryu karate and introduced it to Japan, where it has become one of the four major styles of Japanese karate. The system was directly influenced by the naha-te and shuri-te styles of Okinawan karate.

◀ Rated America's number-one kata champion five consecutive times, Hidy Ochiai is probably most famous for his thrilling exhibitions. He also runs one of the largest karate studios in the United States today.

Who is famous for his extremely high jumping kicks?

Korean karate expert Jhoon Rhee of Washington, D.C. While in his athletic prime, Rhee used to perform a seven-foot jumping front kick while breaking boards, concrete, or tiles held at that height. Since Rhee has stopped giving such exhibitions, Berkeley's Byong Yu has become famous for his aerial breaking acrobatics.

Who is the most famous exponent of aikido today?

Tokyo's Koichi Tohei, a direct student of aikido founder Morihei Uyeshiba. Tohei has given demonstrations of his art throughout the world in an effort to increase interest in his self-defense art.

What is Thomas LaPuppet's full-time occupation?

The former Top 10–ranked karate fighter and Black Belt Hall of Fame member is a fireman by profession.

Who was the first martial-arts personality to appear on the cover of the now-defunct *Action Karate Magazine?*

There were two of them. Steve Sanders was shown executing a side kick which was blocked by his opponent, Carlos Bunda. The photo was taken during the 1968 California Karate Championships in San Francisco.

Who appeared on the first cover of *Karate Illustrated Magazine?*

Texan J. Pat Burleson and Californian Pat Johnson.

Who appeared on the first cover of *Official Karate Magazine?*

New York's John Kuhl was shown demonstrating a flying front kick at Joe Kelleher. The first issue was published in June 1969.

Who appeared on the first cover of *Professional Karate Magazine?*

Publisher Mike Anderson, in promoting his inaugural issue, placed several prominent fighters on his first cover. Among them were world middleweight champ Bill Wallace of Memphis pitted against Texan Roy Kurban, and California's Byong Yu performing a flying side kick over the head of Minnesota's Pat Worley.

Who was the first personality to appear on the cover of *Black Belt Magazine?*

Aikido artist Koichi Tohei appeared on the January 1964 cover. Up to that point, most covers were composed of groups of pictures. The first American martial artist to appear on *Black Belt's* cover was Gene LeBell, who demonstrated a judo throw on the March/April 1964 issue.

Besides writing a classic book on the art of karate, what other achievements is Los Angeles' Hidetaka Nishiyama noted for?

Other than being co-author of *Karate: The Art of Empty Hand Fighting,* a best seller in its field, Nishiyama was responsible for establishing the All America Karate Federation (AAKF) in 1961, and he has served as its president since then. Sanctioned by the Japan Karate Association, the organization is headquartered in Los Angeles and has branches throughout the United States. Primarily, the AAKF oversees the teaching of the shotokan system of karate.

Also in 1961, Nishiyama founded the All America Karate Championships, a tournament open only to members of the AAKF. To date, it is the largest annual tournament among Japanese karate stylists in the United States. The tournament committee is composed of the representatives of the four major styles of Japanese karate: shotokan, goju-ryu, wado-ryu, and shito-ryu. There are no belt divisions in the tourney, and only qualified green, brown, and black belts may enter.

Nishiyama is widely known to be an excellent teacher, having produced a strong body of students. Before coming to America, he competed in his homeland of Japan, becoming one of the earliest All-Japan champions, the most important competitive karate title in Japan.

Who is the president of the All America Karate Federation?

Hidetaka Nishiyama. According to a spokesman, Nishiyama's AAKF is one of the largest karate organizations in the United States. It is chiefly composed of practitioners of the shotokan style of karate.

Who heads the U.S. Goju-Kai?

Gosei Yamaguchi runs the karate association out of his headquarters in San Francisco. It is the principal union of goju-ryu practitioners in the United States.

Who is president of the United States Karate Association?

Veteran Robert Trias of Phoenix, Arizona. According to Trias, the USKA was the first karate organization established in America (1948), and it has grown remarkably to become one of the largest and most widespread associations in the United States.

Who is Jerome Mackey?

Mackey is the president of a controversial chain of judo and karate schools in New York City. He was one of the first American martial artists to own a chain of martial-arts schools where he hired top-level karate and judo instructors for teaching.

Why is Ed Parker considered a showman?

Parker has a dramatic flair for presenting first-class martial-arts demonstrations. Not only does he possess rare skill in the presentation of the physical parts of his demo, but also, his meticulous and sometimes humorous explanations of his craft easily carry the message across to the laymen in the audience. Parker has been called the originator of the "Hollywood" karate exhibition.

Who founded the Uechi-ryu style of karate?

Kanbum Uechi (1868–1947) founded Uechi-ryu karate. It is said that he went to China in 1901 to study kenpo and returned years later to found his style in Okinawa. The style was introduced to the United States by George Mattson of Boston.

Who is the most anonymous man in karate?

It's been said that prominent karate sportswriter Bob MacLaughlin of Los Angeles is the most anonymous because, as editor of several martial-arts magazines, including *Black Belt* and *Professional Karate,* his work was always performed behind the scenes. Mention of his name often brings forth replies such as, "I know I've heard of him somewhere."

Who is the most publicized karate practitioner?

Discounting the late Bruce Lee, who obviously received far more publicity

David Carradine (right) led the *Kung Fu* TV series to a number-one rating in 1973. Recently, he was signed to star in *The Silent Flute,* a film originally scripted by Stirling Silliphant for Bruce Lee.

than any of his colleagues, Chuck Norris has perhaps achieved the most world-wide exposure. Because of his easygoing personality and clean image, Norris has been a favorite with the press ever since his competitive days back in the 1960s. He is best known for his co-starring role in Lee's *Return of the Dragon;* his classic fight scene with Lee in the Roman Colosseum has made Chuck Norris a world-wide household name.

Who was Chin Gempin?

Gempin was a naturalized Japanese subject, originally from China, who died in

1671. Some historians consider him the founder of jujutsu in Japan. However, there exists no proof to substantiate these claims. It is known that Gempin taught some techniques such as atewaza (striking techniques) and Chinese kenpo to ronin (masterless samurai). These ronin later founded their own schools of jujutsu.

Who is Ogawa Ryuzo?

One of Brazil's pioneers of judo, Ogawa Ryuzo immigrated there in 1934 to found the Brazilian Budokan, which has produced a number of Brazilian champions. At age ninety, Ogawa received his 9th-degree black belt.

Bong Soo Han rocketed to national attention for his portrayal of the martial arts in fight scenes in *Billy Jack* and *The Trial of Billy Jack*. Who is his instructor?

Hapkido pioneer Yong Sul Choi of Korea.

Who is the founder of the intricate Korean style of hapkido?

Yong Sul Choi. Choi studied aiki-jutsu ("harmony art," a branch of jujutsu) and tai to-ryu in Japan. He later returned to Korea to found his own art, which he called hapkido.

Which famous tennis star is also a student of karate?

Jimmy Connors. Connors began his study of karate in late 1975 under Emil Farkas of Beverly Hills, California.

Which U.S. Senator used karate to campaign for reelection?

Senator Milton Young of North Dakota, a student of Jhoon Rhee. Young, seventy-seven, won his reelection to a fifth term despite critics' claims that he was too old by publicizing his karate skills. Photographs of the Senator in action—kicking, punching, and jumping—inspired such confidence in his vitality that North Dakotans reelected him.

Who was named "Man of the Century" in the martial arts?

Jhoon Rhee of Washington, D.C. "Man of the Century" was the theme of the

1976 meeting of the Touchdown Club Bicentennial Sports Tribute in Washington. Master of ceremonies Bob Hope presented awards to the most outstanding athletes in eight fields of athletic endeavor. One of those fields was described as "not natively American but one which is becoming more and more a part of the American scene—karate, or more properly the martial arts, of which karate is but one of several forms."

Thus, they named Rhee "Man of the Century in the Martial Arts." He was especially cited for his efforts to broaden the competitive aspects of karate by developing and producing a line of foam-rubber protective gear which permits all-out fights without injury. Rhee received his award along with other sports greats such as boxing's Muhammad Ali, horse racing's Eddy Arcaro, basketball's Wilt Chamberlin, football's Jim Brown, and baseball's Joe DiMaggio.

Are there any practicing black belts who are also handicapped?

Yes. There were four of them until Rhode Island's Ralph Bomba died of cancer in 1975. The other three are Victor Moulton of Plymouth, Massachusetts, who lost part of his left arm in an explosion; Ted Vollrath of Harrisburg, Pennsylvania, a double leg amputee; and Preston Carter of Trenton, New Jersey, a paraplegic.

Who were known as the "dynamic duo" of karate?

The Wilder Twins of New York City. The twin brothers, Calvin and Melvin, received their training from George Cofield and Thomas LaPuppet at the Tong Dojo. They became well known on the East Coast for their fast-paced and entertaining demonstrations. In form exhibitions, their moves were so flawlessly synchronized and they looked so much alike that spectators used to remark how one was a mirror image of the other.

Bruce Lee

If one were to combine the personal contributions of all other martial artists the world over, the results probably wouldn't even come close to the impact Bruce Lee achieved in popularizing the martial arts. The effects of his influence were especially felt in the Orient. The Big Boss, *his first film, which was later released in the United States as* Fists of Fury, *grossed 3.2 million Hong Kong dollars, surpassing* The Sound of Music, *which had held the record at $2.8 million. It also broke box-office records in the Philippines, Singapore, Malaysia, and other parts of Asia.*

When his second movie, called Fists of Fury *in the Orient (*The Chinese Connection *in the United States) hit Hong Kong theaters, it established another record, outgrossing* The Big Boss *by $1.3 million. In the Philippines,* Fists of Fury *ran for over six months, and the government finally had to limit the number of foreign-film imports to protect the domestic producers. In Singapore, scalpers were getting $45 for a $2 ticket. On opening night, hundreds of movie patrons rushed to the theater, causing such a massive traffic jam that the premiere had to be postponed for a week until the authorities could find a way to resolve the problem.*

Then, Way of the Dragon (Return of the Dragon *in the United States),* Lee's *third film venture, went on to establish yet another record: $5.4 million.* Enter the Dragon, *Lee's final film effort for Warner Bros., was a worldwide sensation. Surpassed only by* My Fair Lady, *it was the second-biggest money-maker for Warners in their foreign-distribution history, grossing more than 14 million U.S. dollars. In the United States and Canada alone, it grossed $6.5 million. According to its director, Robert Clouse, Warner Bros. intends to showcase the film in theaters periodically as a perennial classic, much like* Gone with the Wind, *instead of releasing it for television broadcast.*

Bruce Lee (1940–1973)

Bruce's legacy is profound. The colorful, at times controversial king of the martial arts will be discussed for generations, from his humble beginnings at a kung-fu school in Seattle, Washington, to his status as the first Oriental actor to become an international superstar. Unquestionably, there has never been anyone quite like Bruce Lee. And it's certain that there never again will be. It is almost with embarrassment that the authors present only a single chapter on the person who has influenced the martial arts so much. For surely, his deeds deserve volumes. With respect, we dedicate the following to Bruce's widow, Linda, and his children, Brandon and Shannon.

What was Bruce Lee's real name?

His formal name was Lee Jun Fan. His stage name, given him at an early age, was Lee Siu Lung, meaning "Little Dragon."

From whom did Bruce Lee learn kung-fu?

At age thirteen, Lee began training with Yip Man of Hong Kong. The style he learned was called wing-chun.

Where was Bruce Lee born and raised?

He was born in San Francisco in 1940 but was reared in Hong Kong. He returned to the United States at eighteen to attend the University of Washington.

How was Bruce Lee discovered?

During his demonstration at the 1964 International Karate Championships, Lee impressed Hollywood hair stylist Jay Sebring. Sebring later suggested to television producer William Dozier that he use Lee for the co-starring role of Kato in Dozier's *Green Hornet* series.

Who were some of Bruce Lee's celebrity students?

Steve McQueen, Kareem Abdul Jabbar (who appeared in Lee's unfinished *Game of Death*), James Garner, James Franciscus, James Coburn, John Saxon, Van Williams (of the *Green Hornet* series), Academy Award-winning screenwriter Stirling Silliphant, Dean Martin, the late Sharon Tate, and producer Roman Polanski.

Was Bruce Lee the best martial artist in America?

The "best" is like the "most beautiful"—it's all in the eyes of the beholder. There is no question that Bruce Lee was superb in all three levels of combat—the physical, psychological, and academic levels—and he certainly was the best-known martial artist in the entire world. Whether or not he was the best in actual performance can only be answered by those who knew and trained with him. Since Bruce had no interest in competing in tournaments, there is no competitive measuring stick by which to judge him. Nonetheless, he was an advocate of full-

At the 1964 Internationals in Long Beach, Bruce Lee performed so impressively that it led to his co-starring role in the *Green Hornet* series. Above, he's seen demonstrating his famous 1-inch punch which could send opponents reeling backward for more than 6 feet.

contact combat long before it was fashionable in America, and many of the karate champions came to him for instruction.

How long was the *Green Hornet* series on the air?

The *Green Hornet* series began to air on September 9, 1966, and stopped on March 17, 1967. There were twenty-six half-hour episodes in color. Reruns began in 1968. Then it went into local syndication markets. In 1975, a composite of several episodes was released as a feature film in theaters across the the United States.

How did the *Green Hornet* series originate?

Originally, the Green Hornet and his sidekick, Kato, were comic-book heroes of the 1930s. The characters were created by Gene Trendle. Executive producer William Dozier decided to transfer the characters to a television series on the heels of his success with Batman.

What was the name of the specially designed automobile driven by Bruce Lee in the *Green Hornet* series?

Black Beauty, as it was dubbed, was the supercar used in the series. After the series expired, the expensive auto was placed on display at customized-car shows.

What was the offer Hong Kong filmmaker Run Run Shaw made to Bruce Lee in 1970?

While Bruce was on vacation in Hong Kong, Shaw, who operates Asia's largest production company, offered him the standard Asian contract actor's wages: a six-year deal amounting to $75 per week. Later, following Lee's phenomenal success, Shaw was quoted in an interview as stating, "He was just another actor. Who knew?"

But in 1972, when Lee became king of the martial-arts film market, Shaw changed his tune, offering him an estimated $250,000 for a single film. Lee countered, demanding close to $400,000, and Shaw accepted. But the film was never made because of Lee's untimely death.

Was Bruce Lee a child actor?

Yes. Lee made his screen debut in a Hong Kong film called *The Beginning of a Boy* when he was six years old. After that, he played twenty childhood film roles, and he later made a film at eighteen. Interestingly, his earliest debut was really made when he was carried in front of the cameras at the age of three months. All of his early films were made in Hong Kong.

Did Bruce Lee ever win any competitive championships?

Yes, the Inter-School Boxing Championship in Hong Kong shortly after taking up the martial arts. Surprisingly, though, for someone known as a tremendously skilled fighter, he also won the Crown Colony cha-cha championships in 1958.

Who was Bruce Lee's father?

Lee Hoi Chuen, a famous actor-comedian in the Chinese opera.

What was Bruce Lee's rank in the martial arts?

He claimed none. Bruce once said, "I don't have any belt whatsoever. Unless you can really do it, that belt doesn't mean anything. I think it might be useful to hold your pants up."

Did Bruce Lee receive any formal acting training before tackling the role as Kato in the *Green Hornet* series?

Yes, but it was not exactly what you could call comprehensive. Lee's experience in Hong Kong-made films during his youth hardly provided enough professional background. For the Kato role, he was given a one-month crash course with acting instructor Jeff Corey.

Before the *Green Hornet* series, what was the planned TV series in which producer William Dozier intended to cast Bruce Lee?

It was to be a remake of the *Charlie Chan* series, starring Ross Martin of *Wild Wild West* fame. Dozier hired Lee to play Chan's number-one son. The networks were insisting, however, that Dozier's successful *Batman* run for a full season before beginning any new production. In the interim, Dozier replaced the proposed series with the *Green Hornet* series.

What were some of the TV series in which Bruce Lee made little-known appearances?

Immediately after the *Green Hornet* series, Lee made guest appearances on *Blondie*, *Ironside*, and *Here Come the Brides*. A few years later, he co-starred with James Franciscus, his martial-arts student, in four episodes of *Longstreet*.

How much did Bruce Lee receive for his first two Hong Kong films?

The late idol got $7,500 each from producer Raymond Chow for starring in *The Big Boss* (*Fists of Fury* in the United States) and *The Chinese Connection*. He then went into partnership with Chow for their subsequent film ventures.

Who was originally slated to play the lead role on the *Kung Fu* television series?

Bruce Lee. Warner Bros. had a show under consideration in 1970 which ultimately became the *Kung Fu* series. Lee was interviewed for the starring role, but because this was before he had become one of the biggest box-office stars in the world, he wasn't given serious consideration. Some agents and producers felt his English wasn't clear enough and that he wasn't enough of a name to carry the show. Lee, of course, later proved them wrong when he became the first Oriental ever to star in an American-made film—*Enter the Dragon,* produced by none other than Warner Bros.

Why did Bruce Lee use strange yells during the fighting in his films?

Lee's distinctive kiai (pronounced *key*-eye), meaning a yell or scream, was almost like the cry of a cat or a bird. It was specially developed for use in his movies, as Lee had never actually practiced the sounds in his regular workouts.

What kind of nunchaku did Bruce Lee use in his movies?

The special nunchaku (nun-*chaw*-koo) was made of soft polyethylene. The chain connecting the two sticks was made of plastic. Lee was thus able to add realism to his films by using actual contact. Had he used the real hardwood sticks connected by a nylon cord, he would have been unable to produce the realistic effects intended.

Where did Bruce Lee learn to use the nunchaku?

Contrary to many claims, Lee was taught the basic movements of the weapon by Dan Inosanto, who was later to become Lee's student and chief disciple upon his death. Inosanto first demonstrated the moves of the nunchaku to Bruce at the 1964 International Karate Championships in Long Beach, California.

Did Bruce Lee write an early book on kung-fu before he developed his personal style of jeet kune do?

Yes. He wrote his first book back in 1963. It was entitled *Chinese Gung-Fu: The Philosophical Art of Self-Defense.* The book was published by Oriental Book Sales of Oakland, California, a company owned by the late James Y. Lee, Bruce's student, who died shortly before his instructor in 1972. At that time, the company suspended operation. However, the book had already been out of print for several years before James Lee's death and is considered a very rare collector's item.

Did Lee write any other books?

During his short lifetime, Lee was constantly compiling notes for his definitive *Tao of Jeet Kune Do,* the bible of the personal style of combat he founded. In 1975, Linda Lee released the manuscript to Ohara Publications, and it was published later that year. The book contains Lee's personal notes in his own writing and illustrations drawn in his own hand.

Was there an unfinished film Lee planned to do other than *Game of Death?*

Indeed there was. In 1970, he got together with two of his celebrity students, James Coburn and screenwriter Stirling Silliphant, to work on a movie entitled *The Silent Flute.* Pre-production problems plagued the group when they couldn't agree on shooting locations. Warner Bros. wanted at least one setting in India, but Coburn was stubbornly opposed to it. They consequently dropped the project. According to latest reports, the script is still up for sale.

What was one of Bruce Lee's major physical problems?

Lee had a continual problem with undesirable weight loss. Several times a day he would indulge in a specially concocted protein or vegetable drink. The protein drink consisted of Real Blair Protein powder, vegetable oil, peanut flour, powdered milk dissolved in ice water, eggs and their shells, and sometimes bananas. His vegetable drink included carrots, apples, and celery prepared in an electric juicer.

What type of cars did Bruce Lee drive?

Lee enjoyed fast, expensive cars and, true to his nature, he drove them with abandon and panache. While living in Southern California he drove a Porsche; in Hong Kong, a Mercedes 350 SL. Shortly before his death he had on order a brand-new gold Rolls-Royce Corniche.

Who was named "Protector of San Francisco"?

Bruce Lee. Upon his birth on November 27, 1940, his mother, Grace Li, named him Lee Yuen Kam. Since Lee was born in the United States, his mother had used the Americanized spelling of Li. The name meant "Protector of San Francisco," his place of birth. His formal name was later changed for various reasons to Lee Jun Fan. The name Bruce was given him by a nurse in the hospital.

From which U.S. high school did Bruce Lee graduate?

Edison Vocational High School in Seattle, Washington. Lee had started his high-school education in Hong Kong and continued in America when he moved here at age eighteen.

Where was Bruce Lee's first martial-arts school located?

The Jun Fan Gung-Fu Institute was located in a basement in Seattle's Chinatown. The title was a form of Lee's Chinese name, and it more or less read "Bruce Lee's Gung-Fu Institute."

Who was one of the earliest advocates of full-contact martial arts training in the United States?

Bruce Lee developed certain theories along full-contact lines back in 1966 when he founded his personal style of combat—jeet kune do, or "way of the intercepting fist." Because much of the martial arts in America were then noncontact, with techniques pulled short of actual contact, Lee referred to them as comparable to "swimming on dry land."

How did Bruce Lee describe his films?

In an interview, Lee was quoted as saying the following: "I don't play the superhero. But the audience wants to make me one. I don't always play the same kind of role. Each role is different, although when I fight, I come out the same—like an animal.

"I never depend solely on my fighting skill to fulfill any of my film roles, although the audiences in Southeast Asia seem to think so. I believe it is more my personality and the expression of my body and myself. I am not acting. I am just doing my thing. When somebody tries to mimic my battle cries or grimaces, he makes himself look ridiculous.

"There are two types of actors—the versatile one who can go from character to character, and then there is the kind who is typecast, like Clint Eastwood, John Wayne, and Charles Bronson. I see myself as lying somewhere between the two. I am a personality and each role I play shares a bit of that personality.

"I don't call the fighting in my films violence. I call it action. Any action film borders somewhere between reality and fantasy. If I were to be completely realistic, you would call me a bloody violent man. I would simply destroy my opponent by tearing him apart or ripping his guts out. I wouldn't do it so artistically. See, I have this intensity in me, then all is well.

"I didn't create this monster—all this gore in Mandarin films. It was there before I came. At least I don't spread violence. There is always justification for it. A man who has killed many people has to take the responsibility for it. What I am trying to prove is that a man living by violence dies by violence.

"But violence is there in our society. In a way I perhaps anesthetize violence by the way I move my body so that the audience calls it, not violence, but body control.

"I believe that I have a role here in Southeast Asia. The audience needs to be educated and the one to educate them has to be somebody who is responsible. We are dealing with the masses and we have to create something that will get through to them. We have to educate them step by step. We can't do it overnight. That's what I am doing right now. Whether I succeed or not remains to be seen. But I don't just *feel* committed, I *am* committed."

What was Lee's concept for his unfinished film *Game of Death?*

Lee wanted to bring together for the first time a legion of the greatest fighters and athletes in the world to co-star in one film. But *Game of Death* was left unfinished when Lee died. Lee, without even a script, was shooting one week of film footage when his friend and student Kareem Abdul-Jabbar arrived in Hong Kong for other business. Lee enticed the basketball star to work on his film, and the week's footage contained some of the most sensational fight scenes ever filmed. Stills of that fight scene have been converted to posters and marketed all over the world. *Game of Death* actually started in 1973, but was first interrupted when Lee got the offer from Warner Bros. to do *Enter the Dragon.*

How did Bruce Lee die?

According to Professor R. D. Teare, the professor of forensic medicine at the University of London who testified at the coroner's hearing in Hong Kong, "The cause of death was acute cerebral edema [brain swelling] due to hypersensitivity to either meprobamate or aspirin, or possibly the combination of the two, contained in the drug Equagesic." Lee had been given an Equagesic tablet shortly before he had lapsed into permanent unconsciousness on July 20, 1973.

What was unusual about Bruce Lee's funeral?

He had two of them, one in Hong Kong for his friends and fans, and a more private funeral at the Butterworth Mortuary when he was eventually buried in Seattle, Washington.

By which nickname was Bruce Lee known in Hong Kong?

He was called "the man with three legs" because audiences were so impressed by his demonstration of speed in a particular kicking combination of three separate kicks as demonstrated in his film *Fists of Fury* (*The Chinese Connection* in the United States).

How many people appeared at Bruce Lee's funeral in Hong Kong?

An estimated 20,000 assembled outside the Kowloon Funeral Parlor to pay their last respects to the superstar. He was laid out in an open bronze casket.

Who served as pallbearers at Bruce Lee's Seattle funeral?

Superstars Steve McQueen and James Coburn, who were his students and friends; Lee's protégé Dan Inosanto; his brother, Robert Lee; his students Taky Kimura and Peter Chin.

At Bruce Lee's Hong Kong funeral, a banner was placed above his picture. How did it read?

Translated from Chinese, it read "A Star Sinks in the Sea of Art."

What song was played at Bruce Lee's Hong Kong funeral?

A Chinese dirge which resembles "Auld Lang Syne" was played by a band upon the arrival of mourners.

Which songs were played at Bruce Lee's Seattle funeral?

As Bruce wished, the music wasn't traditional. Recordings were played which included the Blood, Sweat and Tears version of "When I Die" (Lee's favorite song), Frank Sinatra's "My Way," Sergio Mendez' "Look Around," and Tom Jones's "The Impossible Dream."

Where is the site of Bruce Lee's grave?

The late martial-arts star was buried at Lake View Cemetery overlooking Lake Washington outside Seattle. Admirers visit by the hundreds, and fresh flowers are continually placed at his grave.

Was Bruce Lee really as proficient in the martial arts as he looked in his movies?

He was a phenomenal martial artist with natural athletic abilities. For instance, he could observe any technique and within a short time, he could perform it flawlessly. Then he would modify it to increase its efficiency. To clarify that statement, consider the following: Lee originally trained *only* in the classical wing-chun style of kung-fu, a system which chiefly concentrates on the use of hands in combat. And yet, claiming no other instructor, Lee was able to add to his fighting arsenal many types of conventional standing kicks as well as the more acrobatic jumping kicks. And it has been repeatedly stated that he taught himself by merely watching other martial artists perform!

As karate pioneer Ed Parker said in describing him, "He was one in two million," meaning that his degree of natural skill was exceptionally rare.

How did Bruce Lee feel women should defend themselves when attacked?

When it came to women, Bruce had no illusions about their ability to defend themselves against an attacker, particularly if a bigger and stronger attacker. "I advise any female learning gung-fu that if they are ever attacked to hit 'em in the groin, poke 'em in the eyes, kick 'em on the shins or the knee . . . and run like hell," he once told a reporter.

What is jeet kune do?

Jeet kune do (jeet coon *doe*), or "way of the intercepting fist," is a collection of basic mental and physical concepts, observations of combat maneuvers, and philosophies of attitude gathered and developed by the late Bruce Lee. His personal fighting method superseded his former practice of the wing-chun style of kung-fu.

a.

In an unrehearsed sparring session with Bob Wall behind the scenes of *Enter the Dragon,* Bruce Lee squares off (a), delivers a spinning back kick (b), closes the gap (c) to execute a front thrust kick (d).

b.

c.

d.

Martial Arts in Television and Movies

Martial arts have been around for thousands of years, while movies and tele-vision are relative newcomers. But with the arrival of the visual media, martial arts had a chance to be seen not just by their practitioners, but also by the millions of laymen who would have otherwise known little about them. Bruce Lee's characters, Billy Jack, James Bond, and countless others are responsible for bringing the martial arts to heights of popularity they never before realized, while simultaneously introducing another side of the arts—entertainment value.

TV's Kung Fu kicked its way into the living rooms of Americans, reaching high network ratings; the movie Billy Jack grossed millions of dollars; and, of course, Bruce Lee became an international superstar via his colorful use of the martial arts in moviedom.

Because of the wide exposure and great potential of the martial arts in the visual media, there are many questions that movie and TV fans and devotees would like to have answered, and this chapter was written for them.

Who was the first martial artist ever to appear on television?

Although it is not not officially known who was first, both Ed Parker and Bruce Tegner appeared in a multitude of TV shows back when U.S. karate was still in its infancy. During the 1950s, Tegner attracted attention to the martial arts by appearing on *Ozzie & Harriet* and *The Detectives,* both of which highlighted karate and made its existence known to the general public. Also during that time, Parker worked with actor Rick Jason on a show called *Case of the Dangerous Robin,* and he also co-starred in a segment of the *I Love Lucy* show which was entirely devoted to karate.

Who was the first martial artist ever to appear in a movie?

James Cagney, a certified judo black belt, demonstrated his expertise on film back as far as 1942. In the late 1950s, Ed Parker and Bruce Tegner both made brief appearances in several films, principally in the capacity of fight-scene coordinators who took part in the fight scenes by doubling for the actors.

Displaying perfect form, hapkido master Bong Soo Han employs a roundhouse kick to deter one of the attackers in the film *The Trial of Billy Jack.* Han's fight-scene choreography in the first *Billy Jack* film helped greatly to popularize the martial arts.

Who served as the first martial-arts choreographer for fight scenes?

Many martial artists, including Ed Parker, Bruce Tegner, and Gordon Doversola, set up fight scenes as early as the late 1950s. However, the first choreographed fight scene to really catch the attention of the public and critics alike appeared in *Billy Jack*. The fights were staged by Korean hapkido expert Bong Soo Han, who also doubled for the film's star, Tom Laughlin. This was the first motion picture in which the use of the martial arts made a significant difference in box-office receipts. Prior to *Billy Jack,* the martial arts were usually presented superficially, making little contribution to the overall success of the films in which they were used.

Did David Carradine actually do his own fighting on the television *Kung Fu* series?

David Carradine seldom did any fighting that called for any expertise. Kung-fu instructor Kam Yuen served as Carradine's double in many of the episodes.

Karateka Bob Wall is perhaps best known for his co-starring role in *Enter the Dragon*. Has he worked in any other films?

Bob also co-starred in Bruce Lee's *Return of the Dragon* and made a brief appearance in Warner Bros.' *Black Belt Jones,* a movie in which he also served as fight-scene choreographer. Wall was the only man ever to co-star in two of the late Bruce Lee's films.

Who was the technical adviser for the fight scenes in the James Bond adventure *You Only Live Twice?*

Donn Draeger, the prolific author of the finest research books in the martial arts, was the film's choreographer. Away from the typewriter, Draeger is a highly competent practitioner of both judo and karate.

Is it true that Sean Connery holds a black belt in karate?

Connery, who starred as James Bond in six of the Bond adventures, was awarded an honorary black belt from Japan's celebrated karate master Mas Oyama. Connery studied briefly with Oyama during the filming of *You Only Live Twice* in 1967. The honorary black belt was given to Connery for his promotion of karate through the film medium, not for his expertise.

Donn Draeger, a former U.S. Marine Corps major who is a master of many Japanese martial arts, instructs Sean Connery in jojutsu, the Japanese sport of stick-fighting, for Connery's role in the James Bond adventure *You Only Live Twice*.

Elvis Presley used to appear to use karate in his films. Is he an authentic practitioner?

A long-time black belt and karate enthusiast, Presley began his study of the art back in 1958 with the late Hank Slemansky, who was killed on active duty in Vietnam. Since then, Elvis has trained with Red West, his chief of security; with Californian Ed Parker, who eventually promoted Elvis to 8th-degree black belt; and, more currently, with world middleweight champion Bill Wallace of Memphis.

Chuck Norris is best known as a former karate champion. Has he also done film work?

Norris has been deeply into acting ever since his co-starring role with the late Bruce Lee in *Return of the Dragon*. At the time of this writing, he had recently completed two movies—one in the United States, the other in Europe. The former, tentatively titled *Cindy Joe and the Texas Turnaround,* is an action-adventure film scheduled for release in 1977.

Veteran actor John Saxon rehearses a fight scene with Bruce Lee for the film *Enter the Dragon*. Saxon had trained in karate many years prior to his starring role in this motion picture.

James Caan rehearses a fight scene for the film *Killer Elite*. Caan spent many months studying the various martial arts necessary for his role.

Does veteran actor John Saxon really study karate?

Saxon began practicing karate long before it became a household word. He started his training under Los Angeles' Hidetaka Nishiyama in the early 1960s and was able to advance to the rank of brown belt, which is the level just below black belt. Because of his hectic film schedules, Saxon has only been able to practice karate irregularly. Since his initiation, he has received additional instruction from Bob Wall, from Hollywood kung-fu instructor Jimmy Woo, and also from the late Bruce Lee during the making of *Enter the Dragon*, in which Saxon co-starred.

Who are some famous actors studying the martial arts?

James Caan, John Saxon, James Garner, Fred Williamson, William Shatner,

Peter Fonda, Dennis Hopper, Robert Culp, Raymond St. Jacques, Robert Conrad, Rick Jason, the late Nick Adams, Steve McQueen, Bill Smith, Ron Ely, and the late Freddie Prinze.

Did David Carradine actually shave all the hair off his head for his role in the *Kung Fu* series?

For at least one episode, Carradine is reported to have shaved his head. Most of the time when he was doing a flashback scene, he wore a skullcap over his head to make him appear bald.

Where can one write to David Carradine?

Even though the *Kung Fu* series has been canceled, one can write to Carradine as well as other stars of the show in care of ABC Television, 4151 Prospect Ave., Hollywood, California 90027. Be sure to address the letter to the person intended.

Is it possible to write to Bruce Lee's widow, Linda Lee?

Yes. Address all letters to Linda Lee, c/o Filipino Kali Academy, 23018 S. Normandie, Torrance, California 90510.

Which famous actress, a student of Bruce Lee's, was a victim in the Manson murders?

Sharon Tate, who studied with Lee during the filming of *The Wrecking Crew*, a Matt Helm adventure starring Dean Martin, was killed during the Manson slayings. Another Lee student and close friend, Jay Sebring, was also slain.

What was the first movie in which Jim Kelly appeared?

The handsome black actor got his real start in *Melinda*, one of the first American-made feature films to use the martial arts prolifically.

What are the films Jim Kelly has done to date?

Kelly has either starred in or appeared in *Melinda, Enter the Dragon, Black Belt Jones, Golden Needles, Truck Turner, Three the Hard Way, Hot Potato,* and *Take a Hard Ride.*

Was Jim Kelly really a karate champion before becoming an actor?

Yes. Kelly won the middleweight title of the 1971 International Karate Championships in Long Beach, California. It was Kelly's major claim to competitive fame, since the Internationals is one of the largest elimination tournaments in America. But that same night, Kelly was defeated by Black Karate Federation president Steve Sanders in the runoff for grand championship. Before this, Kelly had accumulated minor West Coast victories, including grand championship titles at the Four Seasons, the Lima Lama Championships, the West Coast Shotokan, and the Golden West Championships. He also won the middleweight crown of the American Tae Kwon Do Championships.

Who are some of the celebrities Jim Kelly has taught?

Kelly has worked with Gloria Hendry for her role in *Black Belt Jones* and Calvin Lockhart for his role in *Melinda*.

How did Gloria Hendry become such a determined karate enthusiast?

Hendry was introduced to karate when she initially studied it under Jim Kelly for her role in *Black Belt Jones*. Later, she began training with prominent karate coach Jerry Smith. An industrious promoter of the martial arts, the beautiful black actress has appeared as a martial artist on numerous television shows, including the NBC syndicated documentary *Secrets of the Martial Arts*.

From whom did Tamara Dobson study karate for her role as Cleopatra Jones?

The tall, leggy actress actually studied hapkido, not karate, from *Billy Jack's* Bong Soo Han. Han taught her privately before the movie and he also choreographed the numerous martial-arts fight scenes in it.

Who is Tak Kubota?

A well-known Hollywood karate instructor, Kubota has also appeared in many films and commercials. His credits include roles in *The Mechanic, Killer Elite, Get Fisk,* and the award-winning *Sensei* (pronounced *sen*-say). As a technical adviser, Kubota has worked behind the scenes in *Goldfinger, Doc Savage, Shaft in Africa,* and *Doll Squad.*

Did Charles Bronson study karate for his role in *The Mechanic?*

Yes. The international superstar trained with Hollywood karate instructor Tak Kubota to sharpen his skills for at least one fight scene in *The Mechanic.*

Does Ron Ely, who played Doc Savage, actually train in karate?

Ely has been training for several years with Tak Kubota.

Who are some of the celebrities Ed Parker has taught?

Parker has taught Elvis Presley, producer Blake Edwards, the late Nick Adams, Robert Culp, Robert Wagner, Audie Murphy, composer Bronislaw Kaper, Joey Bishop, the late Frank Lovejoy, Darren McGavin, Macdonald Carey, Warren Beatty, and Elke Sommer.

Who is the most famous star ever to study karate?

Probably veteran black belt Elvis Presley, who is perhaps closely followed by superstar Steve McQueen. Although Elvis has remained chiefly behind the scenes in his practice of karate, he appeared in a 1975 issue of *People* magazine throwing a kick at world middleweight karate champion Bill Wallace, Elvis' current instructor. McQueen trains privately with veteran referee and former competitor Pat Johnson of California.

Which famous music composer is also a karate student?

Lalo Schifrin, who composed the music for *Mission Impossible* and *Enter the Dragon,* among many other shows and films. Schifrin trains with Emil Farkas of Beverly Hills. The pair are even negotiating to produce future films which will make use of the martial arts.

Which former film critic and noted author studies the martial arts?

Hollywood's Joe Hyams. The husband of talented actress Elke Sommer first donned a gi back in the early 1960s, when he studied with Ed Parker. Hyams wrote the introduction to one of Parker's first books on the subject, *Secrets of Chinese Karate.* Today, Hyams continues his training with Pat Strong, a former student of Bruce Lee's.

By far the most famous celebrity ever to study karate is Elvis Presley, pictured here with one of his instructors, California's Ed Parker. Elvis is also one of the few celebrities ever to attain the rank of black belt legitimately.

Which noted screenwriter is also a long-time martial-arts enthusiast?

Academy Award-winning screenwriter Stirling Silliphant first trained under the guidance of the late Bruce Lee. The man who penned such screen block-busters as *The Towering Inferno* and *The Poseidon Adventure* continued his studies with karate instructor Tak Kubota upon Lee's death.

Does Priscilla Presley hold any rank in karate?

Yes. The lovely ex-wife of Elvis is a certified green belt, having received her

Hollywood's famous motion-picture and television music composer Lalo Schifrin has been a martial-arts enthusiast for many years. He is pictured here with his instructor, Emil Farkas.

early training from Chuck Norris, then Mike Stone. Her kata, or form, performances were flawless in 1972 when she appeared to be practicing karate regularly, and some observers insist that she could probably have won tournament titles in competition against women of her same rank.

Which television show used to feature famous martial artists regularly?

The Thrillseekers, hosted by actor Chuck Connors. The show occasionally devoted entire half-hour segments to some rather hair-raising exhibitions by martial-arts experts. Those making appearances include Tadashi Yamashita (twice), New York's Ron Duncan, and Mike Crain (Karate for Christ) of Chattanooga, Tennessee.

What unique event took place in the movie *Bad Day at Black Rock?*

In one scene, Spencer Tracy, playing the role of a one-armed veteran, used a combination of judo, karate, and jujutsu to defend himself against an attack from Ernest Borgnine. The classic scene, woven into the tight dramatic theme of the highly praised film, not only was an early use of the martial arts in cinema, but also demonstrated how effective these combative disciplines can be as part of the story line.

What is *The Silent Flute* about?

A cooperative venture by Bruce Lee, Stirling Silliphant, and James Coburn which never got off the ground, *The Silent Flute* traced the trials and tribulations of one man's search for the ultimate martial-arts book. The story was to be pure fantasy, and Bruce would have played a number of roles in the actual film. In late 1976, Sandy Howard Productions, a Hollywood-based independent responsible for such hits as *A Man Called Horse,* bought the rights to *The Silent Flute* and signed David Carradine to star in it. Production is expected to begin by mid-1977.

How authentic was the depiction of the martial arts in the *Kung Fu* TV series?

Producer Jerry Thorpe went through some extravagant motions to lend authentic support to his ABC program. For instance, the technical advisers for the fight scenes, Kam Yuen and David Chow, were both veteran martial artists. Numerous other experienced martial artists were also hired to portray certain scenes at the monastery. Most of the hairless monks, either using skullcaps or actually shaved, were played by martial artists instead of bit-part actors. Whether or not the philosophy inherent in the program was actually authentic is questionable, however. Most of the verbal wisdom flowed from the scriptwriter's pen rather than ancient Chinese scriptures.

For what is Angela Mao-Ying famous?

Angela Mao-Ying is the martial-arts movie queen of Hong Kong. Besides co-starring with Bruce Lee in both *Enter the Dragon* and *The Chinese Connection,*

Mao-Ying has starred in *Lady Kung-Fu, Hapkido, Deep Thrust: Hand of Death, Stoner* (with George Lazenby), and *Deadly China Doll*. She also co-starred with American karate pioneer Jhoon Rhee in *When Tae Kwon Do Strikes* (*Sting of the Dragon Masters* in the United States).

Is veteran Japanese actor Toshiro Mifune a devotee of the martial arts?

Japan's famed cinema star practices several Oriental disciplines, especially kendo, the art of fencing. Mifune first rose to stardom in the classic *Seven Sam-*

Academy Award-winning screenwriter Stirling Silliphant is an avid martial-arts enthusiast who first trained with Bruce Lee. Below, he blocks a playful kick from his wife, Tiana, an actress who made her screen debut in *The Killer Elite.*

urai, which later served as the model for the American-made film *The Magnificent Seven.* Mifune is best known for roles portraying a rough samurai warrior, though he is equally acclaimed as a fine, versatile actor.

What was Toshiro Mifune's most famous role?

It is rather difficult to delineate which role earned Mifune the most fame, although critics claim his sensitive portrayal of a samurai warrior in the 1955 Japanese classic *Seven Samurai* established his credentials as an actor of considerable magnitude.

In which American-made movie did Toshiro Mifune display his martial-arts abilities?

In *Red Sun* with Charles Bronson and Ursula Andress, Mifune demonstrated his expertise with both weaponry and empty-hand combat.

Which American-based karate instructor has starred in several Japanese martial-arts films?

California's Tadashi Yamashita, who formerly rocketed to stardom as one of the most talented Oriental weapons performers in America, was discovered by Japanese filmmakers after his two-time appearance in the television *Thrillseekers* series. Following his surprise discovery, Yamashita starred in the Japanese film *The Karate,* and immediately became a celebrity in the land of the rising sun.

Which female celebrities have studied the martial arts?

Peggy Lipton, Cheri Caffaro, Irene Tsu, Gloria Hendry, Tiana Silliphant, Carol Lawrence, Lana Wood, Pam Grier, Honor Blackman and Diana Rigg.

Who is the famous English actress who also wrote a book on women's self-defense?

Honor Blackman, perhaps best known for her role as Pussy Galore in *Goldfinger,* penned *Honor Blackman's Guide to Women's Self-Defense* back in the mid-1960s.

Starlet Irene Tsu demonstrates extraordinary martial-arts ability by executing an almost-vertical side kick. Tsu has used her expertise in various films such as *Paper Tiger* and *Hot Potato* as well as in television shows.

Who starred in the film *Melinda*, and what was its martial-arts significance?

Calvin Lockhart was the star, and *Melinda* was one of the first American-made feature films to use the martial arts extensively as part of the theme. Additionally, the movie marked the screen debut of actor/karateka Jim Kelly.

Some martial-arts actors have performed impossible feats of skill in their films. Do these feats reflect badly on the martial arts?

No. Most viewers realize that props and camera tricks are responsible for the impossible deeds performed in films. However, youngsters exposed to these displays often enroll in martial-arts studios to learn them, then are disappointed when they discover the feats are physically impossible. There is no critical influence, since people attend these films merely to be entertained.

With whom does Isaac Hayes study karate?

Donnie Williams of Duarte, California. Williams, an aspiring actor who has been billed "karate's clown prince," appeared briefly in *Enter the Dragon,* and more prominently in *Black Belt Jones* and *Killer Elite.*

Who teaches karate to Paul Williams?

The famous songwriter studies with Emil Farkas, co-author of this book.

Why did actress Cheri Caffaro begin studying karate?

Caffaro took up karate when *Girls Are for Loving,* a film she was scheduled to star in, required her to perform karate on screen. Following the film, she enjoyed the experience so much she continued her studies with Emil Farkas.

What was "boy wonder" Phil Spector's association with karate?

Spector, the foremost independent record producer of the 1960s, got involved in the martial arts when he hired two black belts, Santy Josol and Victor Lipton, as his bodyguards. He began taking karate lessons from them and eventually opened up a dojo for them in which to teach their craft. After Josol and Lipton quit teaching, U.S. karate champion Mike Stone acted as Spector's bodyguard when the situation arose for his services.

Is Fred Williamson a karate enthusiast?

Williamson has been studying with Emil Farkas of Beverly Hills since 1972. He displayed some of his expertise in the film *That Man Bolt.*

Fred Williamson (left) is one of the many stars who have studied the martial arts with instructor Emil Farkas. Herb Alpert, Dennis Hopper, Raymond St. Jacques, Sheri Caffaro, James Caan, and Peggy Lipton are among Farkas' other celebrity students.

Who are some of the children of celebrities who study the martial arts?

Some of the children infatuated with karate are offspring of Polly Bergen, Mike Connors, Herb Alpert, Buddy Hackett, Jack Carter, Kirk Douglas, and Barry Gordy, Jr.

Which famous trumpet player is also a longtime karate devotee?

An ardent practitioner of karate, Herb Alpert has trained for five years, since 1972, with Emil Farkas.

Which famous martial artist is also a well-known movie stuntman?

Judo and wrestling champion Gene LeBell of Los Angeles has been a stunt coordinator and stuntman since 1955 and has done countless films. LeBell became a member of the Stuntman's Association in the early 1960s. He served as an opponent to Bruce Lee in several memorable fight scenes from the old *Green Hornet* TV series. In addition, LeBell has worked with such stellar celebrities as Elvis Presley, James Caan, Robert Wagner, Jerry Lewis, Bob Hope, Jack Benny, James Whitmore, David Carradine, and Joe Don Baker. Today, he is still as active as ever.

Does Muhammad Ali really practice karate?

The "People's Choice" has been intermittently a practicing advocate of karate for the past four years. In fact, Ali's ex-wife Belinda also studies. Ali began his early karate training with George Dillman of Reading, Pennsylvania. Both he and Belinda are currently under the tutelage of Jhoon Rhee of Washington, D.C. Ali has even engaged in exhibition sparring matches with karate fighters such as Miami's Joe Hess, and, in 1975, a photo of the heavyweight boxing champion wearing a karate uniform and Safe-T equipment appeared in newspapers throughout the world.

Who are some of the noted recording artists who have pursued the study of the martial arts?

The list is long and distinguished: Elvis Presley, Engelbert Humperdinck, Mark Lindsay, Carol Lawrence, Robert Goulet, conductor Bronislaw Kaper, Herb Alpert, Lalo Schifrin, songwriter Paul Williams, David Crosby of Crosby, Stills, Nash and Young, the rock group Foghat, José Feliciano, Richie Havens, Gabor Szabo, prominent ex–record producer Phil Spector, Jeff Barry and Isaac Hayes.

Do prominent sports stars study martial arts?

Yes. In baseball, Roy White, Tony Kubrick, and Steve Arlin; in boxing, Muhammad Ali; in football, Fred Williamson, Jimmy Orr, Roman Gabriel, Pat Mat-

The colorful and controversial world heavyweight boxing champion Muhammad Ali spars with his karate instructor, Jhoon Rhee of Washington, D.C. Rhee invented the Safe-T Equipment worn above by Ali.

son, Bruce Coslet and Bob Geddes; in basketball, Kareem Abdul-Jabbar, Sidney Wicks, and Curtis Rowe; in tennis, Jimmy Connors.

Who is the wealthiest person practicing the martial arts in America?

Beyond a shadow of a doubt, Elvis Presley.

What is director Sam Peckinpah's connection to the martial arts?

Hollywood's veteran filmmaker, who has undertaken projects such as the action-packed *The Wild Bunch,* directed *Killer Elite,* a 1975 motion picture which provided a showcase for martial-arts fight scenes. Appearing in the film were martial artists Emil Farkas, Tak Kubota, Donnie Williams, Eric Lee, Gene LeBell, and Dan Inosanto. James Caan and Robert Duval of *Godfather* fame starred in the film, as well as Tiana Silliphant, wife of Academy Award–winning screenwriter Stirling Silliphant, who penned the script for *Killer Elite.* The movie, boasting a $5 million budget, is the most distinguished motion picture ever to include the martial arts as a part of the story line.

Sam Peckinpah (right) on the set of *Killer Elite,* a film in which some of America's top martial artists appeared. Author Emil Farkas is seen at left dressed as a Ninja assassin.

Books and Publications

Proper use of research material is a stepping stone to professionalism in any endeavor. For that very reason it would be inappropriate in this book to omit a chapter on the printed word. There is a wealth of knowledge to be gained from existing books and publications. The concerned student can use such tools to enhance his regular training and increase his understanding of the martial arts.

In some cases, the serious scholar will want to pore over just about every available publication on the market. Others with less time may prefer simply to be informed of current events. In either case, this chapter will tell you what to look for, and where to go about getting it. For the sake of the earnest devotee, we have delved into some of the more notable collector's items. With a little obstinacy, some of these rare texts can still be procured. And for the historian, the authors have given the backgrounds of some of the foremost publications in the field. Much like the martial arts themselves, the books and publications offer something for everybody.

What was unique about *Action Karate Magazine?*

A defunct publication founded by Ed Parker, the magazine was the first in the United States to attempt to publicize the Americans' viewpoint of karate instead of that of the Oriental instructors. *Action Karate* flourished briefly during the late 1960s. Copies can still be purchased as collector's items by writing Ed Parker, 315 South Beverly Drive, P.H. Suite, Beverly Hills, California 90212.

Some of the many different martial-arts publications from all corners of the world. While some of these publications have appeared only recently, many of them have been around for more than a decade.

What was the first martial-arts magazine in the United States to become permanently established?

Along with several other investors, Mito Uyehara founded *Black Belt Magazine* in 1961. After many ups and downs, Uyehara and his brother, Jim, took over ownership. Today, Mito, the sole owner, heads the Rainbow Publications empire, which also publishes two other martial-arts-related magazines.

Which is the best book written about karate?

Although it was first published way back in 1960, even today Hidetaka Nishiyama's book *Karate: The Art of Empty-Hand Fighting* is considered the unsurpassed work on the subject. The work is unique in that it tells the reader what not to do as well as how to perform various aspects of karate. The photographs, taken from many angles, superbly illustrate the correct form of each technique, and the writing is clear and precise. Co-authored by Richard C. Brown, the book is still available through the Charles E. Tuttle Co. of Tokyo, Japan, and Rutland, Vermont.

Which is the best reference book written about the martial arts?

Asian Fighting Arts, written by Donn Draeger and Robert W. Smith, is universally recognized as the principal authority on the subject. It provides stimulating insights into every major form of combat as well as some minor arts stemming from all of the Asian countries. It was published by Kodansha International, a subsidiary of Harper and Row, in 1969. Today, it is also available in paperback.

Who founded *Inside Kung-Fu Magazine?*

Curtis Wong, a kung-fu practitioner, founded the magazine in 1973. It was the first publication to devote its pages almost totally to kung-fu exponents.

What are the major martial-arts magazines, and where does one subscribe to them?

Black Belt, Karate Illustrated, and *Fighting Stars* magazines are all published

Some of the best-selling martial-arts books in the English language.

by Rainbow Publications, 1845 W. Empire Ave., Burbank, California 91504. Others are *Professional Karate Magazine* and *World Martial Arts Digest,* P.O. Box 20232, Oklahoma City, Oklahoma 73120; *Official Karate Magazine,* Charlton Building, Derby, Connecticut 06418; and *Inside Kung-Fu Magazine,* 7011 Sunset Blvd., Hollywood, California 90028. *Judo Magazine* is published in Sacramento, California. There are numerous bimonthly and quarterly publications on the subject, chiefly published in New York. Two of these "pulp" mags, *Defense Combat* and *Fighting Champions,* come from the same offices as *Official Karate.* The two remaining pulps are *Masters of Self-Defense,* 257 Park Avenue South, New York, New York 10010; and *Fighting Arts,* Can-Am Media Building, 313 West 53rd St., New York, New York 10019.

Are there places from which one can order martial-arts books?

There are several major mail-order companies which handle not only books but martial-arts supplies as well. Among those you can ask for a catalog are the following: Ohara Publications, 1845 W. Empire Ave., Burbank, California 91504; Martial Arts Supply Company, 10711 Venice Blvd., Los Angeles, California 90034; Mantis Supply Company, 7011 Sunset Blvd., Hollywood, California 90028; Castello Combative Sports Company, 836 Broadway, New York, New York 10003; Honda Associates, 485 Fifth Ave., New York, New York 10017; Divine Wind, Inc., Box 4116, Mountain View, California 94040; Black Dragon Fighting Society, P.O. Box A-3727, Chicago, Illinois 60690; the Charles Tuttle Company, Rutland, Vermont 05701; and Kodansha International, 10 East 53rd St., New York, New York 10022.

Check the local Yellow Pages or the martial-arts magazines for advertisements. The above are the recommended companies.

Which is the biggest-selling martial-arts magazine in America?

The audited circulation of *Black Belt Magazine* reached 120,000 copies per month during 1975, the largest known figures in the United States. *Black Belt* can probably attribute the high figures to the format of the mag, which concentrates on a wide spectrum of martial arts, including karate, kung-fu, judo, aikido, and jujutsu, among many others. *Black Belt*'s competitors primarily restrict their coverage to karate and kung-fu.

How did *Black Belt Magazine* come to be the largest?

The mag started out in 1961 and was the very first such publication on the market. Its first issue was in digest form. One of the original investors, Mito Uyehara, came from Hawaii in 1960 to start an aikido school in Los Angeles.

He began writing a small column in a local newspaper to promote aikido and started getting calls to do articles for other local newspapers. Soon after, he decided to publish a magazine, even though he was a certified public accountant by profession. So Mito and his brother, Jim Uyehara, and two other investors put up $500 apiece to start *Black Belt.*

But someone had misinformed them that it would cost only $500 to produce one issue of the magazine. They had therefore figured they had enough for four issues. As it turned out, production and typesetting costs alone amounted to $5,000 per issue and they were unable to pay for the first printing bill. Instead, they gave the printer 5,000 copies and asked him to sell them to cover his costs. The printer pushed them off on a distributor in New York, who sold them like crazy and ordered 25,000 copies of the next issue. The Uyeharas received a $6,000 bill for issue number two and found the going very rough from that point on.

Two years later, in 1963, the Uyeharas were in debt to the tune of $30,000 and nearly closed down. One of Mito's favorite stories concerning that period is how he offered his typewriter, one of the few liquid assets, to debt collectors. Mito and Jim then bought out their partners to give it one last shot. Since the existing karate supply companies would not advertise in the magazine, the Uyeharas started their own supply company. The sister company was so successful that it carried *Black Belt* through '63 and into '64, when it went monthly and finally began to clear a profit.

In 1970, *Black Belt* had maintained its rank as the best-selling magazine in the martial-arts field, but the brothers couldn't agree and split up. Jim took the supply company and Mito the magazine. Today, Mito publishes *Karate Illustrated* and *Fighting Stars* in addition to *Black Belt.* He owns his own building and book-publishing firm, Ohara Publications, which carries about fifty titles in quality softbound books. It is now a multi-million-dollar enterprise.

Is Al Weiss a practitioner of the martial arts?

The prolific editor of *Official Karate, Defense Combat,* and *Fighting Champions* magazines has been practicing karate for the past sixteen years and is a certified black belt. Weiss started his training with New York City's Johnny Kuhl in 1960. He is one of the few editors to hold a black belt.

In which of the martial arts does Mito Uyehara hold black belts?

The publisher and president of Rainbow Publications was practicing and teaching aikido before he moved into his chosen profession. After meeting Bruce Lee around 1966, Mito began studying jeet kune do under the private tutelage of the late martial-arts film idol. He continued once-a-week lessons at Lee's former home in Bel Air, California for about two years.

Which former tournament competitor became a magazine publisher?

Professional Karate Magazine publisher Mike Anderson was formerly a karate competitor, businessman, and instructor before moving into the publishing field. As a competitor, Anderson fought in both Europe and America. He won the All-European Open Championships four times and the U.S. Armed Forces Championships twice while stationed in Europe during the early 1960s. Anderson was the runner-up in the late Pat Wyatt's and Ken Knudson's 1971 Nationals and captain of the Midwest team that competed in the first All-Star Black Belt Championships in California. Anderson reached the zenith of his competitive career by winning the runner-up slot to grand champion Bill Wallace in the 1971 USKA Grand Nationals in, of all places, Anderson, Indiana.

What year was *Karate Illustrated* founded?

The sister publication to *Black Belt* was founded as a bimonthly in 1969. It went monthly in 1973.

What was the first best-selling novel ever to publicize karate?

Ian Fleming's *Goldfinger,* published in 1959, was the first major novel to depict karate as a skill possessed by a prominent character. In it, Goldfinger's assistant, Oddjob, served as a karate-trained bodyguard. The James Bond adventure novel sold millions of copies before being released as a film in 1965.

What are some of the novels dealing with the martial arts?

There are quite a few, most published in the 1970s. One of the first novels to use the martial arts as a principal part of the story line was a book entitled *Judo Boy* by J. Ball, Jr. The book first appeared in the early '60s. The more recent entries are *Karate Is a Thing of the Spirit,* which may be released as a film; *Kung-Fu,* a series of paperback books taken from the television series of the same name; the Jason Striker series of fictional martial-arts adventures; *The Legend of Bruce Lee* by Alex Ben Block; Linda Lee's *Bruce Lee: The Man Only I Knew; The Black Samurai* by Marc Olden; and a martial-arts Western called *Sloan.* The only true adventure story dealing with the use of martial arts is *Tokyo Undercover* by veteran black belt Dan Ivan. The novel depicts Ivan's escapades as an undercover agent in Toyko and Korea with the American military forces after World War II.

Who is the most prolific martial-arts author?

Japan's Donn Draeger has written twenty-eight books dealing with the subject. All of them have been comprehensive, informative and accurate and usually delineate more history and tradition than mere physical technique.

What are some of the best-selling martial-arts books?

Karate: The Art of Empty-Hand Fighting by Hidetaka Nishiyama and Richard C. Brown; *This Is Karate* by Mas Oyama; *Asian Fighting Arts* by Donn Draeger and Robert Smith; *The Illustrated Kodokan Judo; Karate's Basic Principles* by A. Pfluger; *The Sport of Judo* by Kobayashi and Sharp; *Jujitsu Complete* by Kiyoze Nakae; *The Tao of Jeet Kune Do* by Bruce Lee; *Nunchaku: Karate Weapon of Self-Defense* by Fumio Demura; and *White Crane Gung-Fu* by Michael P. Staples.

What is the unique feature of the book *Zen Combat*?

Zen Combat, written by Jay Gluck in 1962, was the first book to act as a complete guide to the different martial arts of Japan. It explains diverse crafts, from karate and aikido to the lesser-known types of stickfighting and other weapons uses. The author also gives many anecdotes about the famous Japanese martial artists as well as a first-hand insight into living legends such as Gogen "The Cat" Yamaguchi and Mas Oyama.

Has Gogen Yamaguchi written a book in the English language?

The legendary "Cat" has indeed authored an English-language work on his goju-ryu karate style, but very few have ever seen it, let alone read it. The voluminous book, published by the International Karate-Do Goju-Kai and entitled *Karate, Goju-ryu*, saw little in the way of distribution because the original photographs were destroyed in a fire at the publisher's offices after the first printing. Rainbow Publications, publishers of *Black Belt Magazine*, among many other books and magazines, somehow ended up with the original brownline. The rare edition includes a lengthy autobiography written by Yamaguchi himself.

What is the best book delineating the development of karate in the United States?

Though some critics tend to think that it was written from the viewpoint of a Japanese stylist, Robin L. Rielly's *The History of American Karate* is the most comprehensive work on the subject. The author published the work himself, and it was distributed in limited quantities in 1970 by the Semper Fi Company, Inc., of Little Ferry, New Jersey. The book, however, sold out its first printing and has since been out of print. It is now considered a valuable collector's item.

What is unusual about Peter Urban's book *The Karate Dojo?*

It was one of the first English-language martial-arts books published, and it contained some very interesting accounts of several legendary karate masters. The marketability of the book speaks for itself; it has been on sale for more than a dozen years.

Which book is considered the "bible of judo"?

The Illustrated Kodokan Judo, published by the Kodokan in 1955. It contains over three hundred pages of informative text with more than a thousand photographs, many of them of Professor Jigoro Kano, the founder of Kodokan judo. Unfortunately, the book is out of print and is a rare collector's item.

Which book was written by Mifune?

The last of the 10th-degree judo black belts authored the famous *Canon of Judo.* Containing more than 250 pages and 1,000 photos, the book was first published in the early 1960s, but is now out of print.

For what is Robert W. Smith noted?

Smith is probably the second most prolific author of martial-arts literature, Donn Draeger being first. Smith was the co-author with Draeger of the comprehensive *Asian Fighting Arts,* the most accurate source about the Oriental fighting disciplines ever written. On his own, Smith wrote *Chinese Boxing: Masters and Methods; Weapons & Fighting Arts of the Indonesian Archipelago; Pa-Kua: Chinese Boxing; Shaolin Temple Boxing;* and *Tai-Chi: The Supreme Ultimate Exercise.* Smith, now living in Maryland, spent many years in the Orient studying various facets of the martial arts. He has also compiled the most exhaustive bibliography of the martial arts ever assembled. It lists books and articles in all major languages and was first published as part of his book *Judo* in the mid-1950s.

How did *Black Belt Magazine* get its name?

Publisher Mito Uyehara chose the appropriate title for two reasons, according to the editorial printed in the first issue. "First, only in the Oriental self-defense arts and sports is the black belt worn as part of the uniform. And then it is worn only by an individual who has achieved the rank of shodan, or first-degree.

"Second, it [the black belt] has a deep significance for all enthusiasts of judo, aikido, karate and kendo. This is because the black belt denotes the expert. The wearer of the black belt is recognized as a qualified instructor."

Today, largely due to the commercialism the martial arts have undergone, the last statement is no longer true, because there are cases of phony instructors who are not really qualified to teach.

Does *Inside Kung Fu Magazine* concentrate only on kung-fu?

No. The magazine which calls itself the "ultimate in martial arts coverage" provides exposure to all of the various arts. The sport aspect is the least covered by the publication.

Did *Professional Karate Magazine* cover only sport karate?

The magazine, which is no longer published, generally concentrated on sport karate activities, but also included articles on other subjects.

Which European martial-arts magazine was popular in the 1960s?

Budo Magazine Europe, published by Judo International out of Paris, France. The publication covered all the different martial arts and had an impressive list of contributing editors.

Are there martial-arts magazines currently published in foreign countries?

Yes. France alone has four such magazines, published in three various languages. They are entitled *Karate, Karateka, Karate Cinema,* and *Judo France.* England has *Combat* and *Fighting Arts.* Hong Kong has a wide spectrum of martial-arts periodicals. The Kodokan also publishes a judo magazine in the Japanese language.

Is there a magazine for women in the martial arts?

Yes. *Black Belt Woman* was first published in September 1975, and at the time of this writing, has three issues out. The publication deals exclusively with the female members of the art and sport. In fact, all of its articles are written by women practitioners. Included are topics on tournaments, philosophy, training aids, self-defense situations, and physiology. Copies can be obtained by writing *Black Belt Woman*, 22 Ashcroft Rd., Medford, Massachusetts 02155.

Who is the largest European distributor of books on the Asian fighting arts?

Judo International of Paris, France. Another large Parisian distributor is Sedirep.

Which major general-interest publications have printed stories on the martial arts and their personalities?

The list is infinite, but some of the major magazines carrying such stories have been *Viva, Penthouse, Esquire, Sports Illustrated, Newsweek, Harper's, Womensports, Playgirl, The National Enquirer, Time, Black Sports, Life, The Wall Street Journal,* and *Players*.

Who for many years served as book reviewer for *Black Belt Magazine*?

Dr. Philip Rasch, an educator and doctor of physical education, submitted in-depth reviews during the 1960s. When Ohara Publications, *Black Belt*'s sister company, was founded the reviews were discontinued.

Who was responsible for the unique covers on early issues of *Black Belt* and *Karate Illustrated*?

Photographer Oliver Pang. To this day, martial-arts advocates still discuss the uniqueness of Pang's cover shots, which combined the finest in photography with artistic design. Pang later suffered from a serious eye defect which unfortunately ended his promising career. Pang kept in his possession most of the negatives of his work, including those of the late Bruce Lee. Nostalgic collectors often attempt to contact him for copies of his photos.

What is *Self-Defense World*?

A small slick-paper magazine published and distributed in limited quantities on the West Coast. It is one of the many house organs published in the "world" category, such as *Runner's World, Cyclist's World,* etc.

Who claims to have the largest martial-arts publication in the world?

French publishing magnate Dominic Nouillhac. Nouillhac publishes thirteen magazines, six of which are devoted to various aspects of the martial arts. According to his demographics, his French-language *Karate* sells 250,000 copies per issue, more than double the sales of America's *Black Belt.*

Which martial-arts publishing firms have also promoted karate events?

Almost all of them. Both *Official Karate* and *Inside Kung-Fu* have produced amateur karate tournaments. Rainbow Publications has promoted both expositions and full-contact karate events. In 1976, French publishing magnate Dominic Nouillhac formed a partnership with *Professional Karate's* Mike Anderson to produce a series of international full-contact events in various parts of the world. The merger was the first such union of international karate publications.

Who compiled the first *Who's Who in the Martial Arts?*

Bob Wall, co-star of two Bruce Lee films—*Enter the Dragon* and *Return of the Dragon.* Wall established strict guidelines for entrance into the *Who's Who,* and after testing the positive accomplishments of more than four hundred martial artists across the United States, 135 members were elected, eleven of whom were women. The book is published by R. A. Wall Investments, Inc., of Beverly Hills and can also be purchased at martial-arts supply companies.

Are there any books on the sport aspect of karate?

Winning Tournament Karate by Chuck Norris is the only one at the time of this writing. It's published by Ohara Publications of Burbank, California.

How has animaction been used in the karate field?

Mike Stone, a legendary karate fighter, did three of these flip books for Ohara Publications. Animaction occurs when a series of still photos placed in sequence are flipped consecutively until the stills appear to unravel much like a film clip. Bob Wall and Jim Kelly also posed for a flip book which was used for promotion of *Enter the Dragon.*

Has a book been written on Chinese kenpo?

Yes. In 1963, Prentice-Hall published *Secrets of Chinese Karate* by Ed Parker.

Which books teach the shotokan style of karate?

There are five major works concentrating on the popular Japanese karate system: Hidetaka Nishiyama's classic *Karate: The Art of Empty-Hand Fighting*, published by Charles E. Tuttle of Tokyo, Japan; Shotokan founder Gichin Funakoshi's massive *Karate-Do Kyohan: The Master's Textbook*, published by Kodansha International of Tokyo, Japan; Tonny Tullener's *Beginning Karate*, published by Ohara Publications of Burbank; *Dynamic Karate: Techniques of Self-Defense* by Masatoshi Nakayama, published by Kodansha International; and *Black Belt Karate* by Jordon Roth.

Are there books about the kyokushinkai style of karate?

Yes. Kyokushinkai (kyoh-*koo*-shin-kye) founder Mas Oyama wrote four books on his popular system: *What Is Karate, This Is Karate, Vital Karate,* and *Advanced Karate.*

Has a book been written on the goju-ryu karate system?

Two of the books on the subject were penned by goju-ryu (*go*-jew-ryoo) founder Gogen Yamaguchi's son, Gosei. They are entitled *Goju-Ryu Karate* and *Goju-Ryu II.*

Has any book ever been printed concerning Bruce Lee's unique method of jeet kune do?

In 1975, Ohara Publications printed the *Tao of Jeet Kune Do,* a collection of the late superstar's martial concepts.

What is the most extensive book written on tae kwon do?

The Korean martial art was comprehensively explained by General Choi Hong Hi in his book *Tae Kwon Do,* published by the Daeha Publishing Co. of Seoul, Korea.

Has anyone written a book on tang soo do?

The Korean martial art was captured on paper by legendary fighter Chuck Norris. Entitled *Basic Karate Fundamentals*, it is currently published by R. A. Wall Investments, Inc., of Beverly Hills.

Is there a book in English on the wado-ryu style of karate?

Cecil Patterson wrote *An Introduction to Wado-Ryu Karate* in 1974 for Ohara Publications.

Is there a book written which combines karate and weight training?

Yes. Co-authors Ron Marchini and Leo Fong, two prominent martial artists and weight-training enthusiasts, combined the best of the two physical cultures in their *Power Training in Kung-Fu and Karate*. The book was published by Ohara Publications.

Which famous out-of-print book is nonetheless a must for all martial-arts students?

The Fighting Spirit of Japan by E. J. Harrison. The work is an esoteric study of the martial arts and the way of life in Japan. The author examines the arts and their effect on the individual both physically and spiritually.

Has anyone ever written an encyclopedia of the martial arts?

There have been many futile attempts made in the past. Ted Kresge of St. Petersburg, Florida, actually completed an encyclopedia, but was unsuccessful in his attempts to self-publish and promote it. There is, however, a comprehensive encyclopedia of the martial arts currently being written by Emil Farkas and John Corcoran, the authors of this book. At this point it is half-completed and is expected to deal with approximately five thousand entries. It already contains Corcoran's four-language dictionary of martial-arts terminology. Once completed, the encyclopedia may very well be considered the ultimate reference book on the subject.

Does Canada have its own martial-arts magazine?

Yes. *Oriental Fighting Arts* has editorial offices at 5871 Victoria, Suite 219,

Montreal, P.Q., Canada, and its business offices are in New York. Strangely enough, the majority of its articles are written about martial artists in the United States.

At one time, there was also a judo publication published by the Canadian Kodokan Black Belt Association.

What is unusual about the editorial offices of *Official Karate Magazine?*

The average reader would never be able to find them. The actual address doesn't appear anywhere in the magazine. Instead, the business and advertising office locations are given. The editorial address is: Galaxy International, 351 West 54th St., New York, New York 10019.

Were there martial-arts magazines published in America prior to *Black Belt* in 1960?

Yes. Bruce Tegner published a magazine called *Judo* back in 1952. Besides judo techniques, the magazine also featured personality stories. It was probably the first such magazine ever distributed in the United States.

Currently, which is the largest book written about a martial art?

Probably, *Tae Kwon Do* by General Choi Hong Hi. The book measures 9½ x 13 inches with more than 3,240 photographs contained in 518 pages. It was published in 1965 by Daeha Publishing Co. of Seoul, Korea.

Can a person learn a martial art from reading books?

It is possible to gain basic knowledge and understanding from reading material, but it would be extremely difficult to learn even the intermediate techniques without the guidance of a qualified instructor. Books are an excellent supplement to training, but they cannot replace actual instruction.

Guide to Martial Arts Nomenclature

aikido (eye-*key*-doe) "way of spirit meeting"; Japanese method of self-defense which took root from a form of jujutsu. It was founded in 1942 by Morihei Uyeshiba.

dan (dawn) "rank" or "degree"; any one of various black-belt ranks in the Okinawan and Japanese martial arts.

dojo (*doe*-joe) "training hall"; an establishment in which the Japanese martial arts are taught.

goju-ryu (*goh*-jew-ryoo) "hard-soft way"; one of the four major Japanese karate systems.

gup (goop) "grade" or "class"; any one of the various grades below black belt in the Korean martial arts.

isshin-ryu (*ish*-in-ryoo) "one-heart way"; a hybrid form of unarmed combat founded in 1955, and based on several Okinawan karate styles.

jeet kune do (jeet coon *doe*) "way of the intercepting fist"; a collection of mental and physical concepts, observations of combat maneuvers, and philosophies of attitude gathered and developed by the late Bruce Lee.

judo (*jew*-doe) "gentle way"; a Japanese method of self-defense developed from jujutsu which incorporates throws, grappling, and some striking techniques.

judogi (*jew*-doe-ghee) "judo uniform"; the outfit worn in judo.

judoka (jew-*doe*-ka) "judo man"; an encompassing term for any judo practitioner.

jujutsu (jew-*jut*-sue) "gentle art"; a generic term applied to several native Japanese methods of unarmed and armed combat.

karate (ka-*raw*-tay) "China hand" or "'empty hand"; a form of unarmed combat which originated in Okinawa after being influenced by earlier Chinese martial arts.

karateka (ka-*raw*-tay-ka)   "karate man"; a practitioner of karate.

kata (*caught*-ah)   "formal exercises"; a routine composed of prearranged martial-arts tactics, which is performed in a manner similar to shadowboxing. This is a Japanese expression. It is called kuen (*koo*-en) in Chinese martial arts, and hyung in Korean styles.

kendo (*ken*-doe)   "sword way"; the modern art of Japanese fencing.

ki (key)   "air" or "breath" or "spirit"; the centralized energy of the body which, through concentration and development of breath, can be applied to accomplish physical feats.

kiai (*key*-eye)   "spirit meeting"; a loud shout of self-assertion.

kung-fu (kung-*foo*)   "skill" or "time" or "task" or "work"; a generic term used in the Western Hemisphere to represent the Chinese martial arts.

kwoon   "training hall"; an establishment in which the Chinese martial arts are taught.

kyokushinkai (kyoh-*koo*-shin-kye)   "extreme truth association"; a hybrid style of Japanese karate founded by Mas Oyama.

kyu (cue)   "grade" or "class"; any one of the various grades below black belt in the Japanese martial arts.

martial arts   an encompassing term for the Asian fighting arts.

ninja (*nin*-ja)   "stealer in" or "spy"; a military spy of feudal Japan.

nunchaku (nun-*chaw*-koo)   one of the five systematized weapons of Okinawa, a wooden flail that was originally a farming tool.

obi (*oh*-bee)   "belt"; the belt worn in the Japanese martial arts.

pankration (pan-*kray*-shin)   "all powers"; an early Greek sport which developed as a combination of earlier forms of boxing and wrestling. It could very well be the first "total" martial art known to man.

sensei (*sen*-say)   "teacher"; an instructor of the Japanese martial arts.

shotokan (*show*-toe-kawn)   "Shoto's house"; one of the four major Japanese karate systems. Its name was taken from the founder's pen name.

sifu (*see*-foo)   "teacher"; a male instructor of kung-fu. A female teacher is called simu (*see*-moo).

sumo (*sue*-mow)   "struggle"; a Japanese form of wrestling in which the participants are of gigantic proportions.

tae kwon do (tay-kwon-*doe*)   "ways of hands and feet"; the term representative of Korean karate.

wado-ryu (*wah*-doe-ryoo)   "way of peace"; one of the four major Japanese karate systems.

Index

[*Italic* page numbers indicate photographs.]